COOKBOOK CLUB

PLANT-BASED RECIPES FOR ENTERTAINING

Shadan Kishi Price

Copyright © 2025 by Shadan Kishi Price

All rights reserved. No portion of this book may be reproduced in any form without written permission from the author, except as permitted by U.S. copyright law.

Any trademarks and/or brands included in this cookbook are the property of their respective owners. No claim is made to them and no endorsement by them is implied or claimed in the following recipes.

Library of Congress Control Number: 2025910525

ISBN (hardcover) 978-1-6653-1082-6
ISBN (paperback) 978-1-6653-1081-9

These ISBNs are the property of BookLogix for the express purpose of sales and distribution of this title. BookLogix is not responsible for the writing, editing, or design/appearance of this book. The content of this book is the property of the copyright holder only. BookLogix does not hold any ownership of the content of this book and is not liable in any way for the materials contained within. The views and opinions expressed in this book are the property of the Author/Copyright holder, and do not necessarily reflect those of BookLogix.

This publication is designed to provide accurate and authoritative information in regard to the subject matter covered. It is sold with the understanding that the author is not engaged in rendering legal, investment, accounting or other professional services. While the author has used their best efforts in preparing this book, they make no representations or warranties with respect to the accuracy or completeness of the contents of this book and specifically disclaim any implied warranties of merchantability or fitness for a particular purpose. No warranty may be created or extended by sales representatives or written sales materials. The advice and strategies contained herein may not be suitable for your situation. You should consult with a professional when appropriate. The author is not liable for any loss of profit or any other commercial damages, including but not limited to special, incidental, consequential, personal, or other damages.

for trey, maman, baba, baharan, joy, and my cookbook club friends

Top shelf

- Persepolis: Vegetarian Recipes from Persia and Beyond
- an edible mosaic — Faith E. Gorsky
- The Middle Eastern Kitchen — Rukmini Iyer
- NADIYA HUSSAIN — TIME TO EAT
- Feast from the Mideast: 250 Sun-Drenched Dishes from the Lands of the Bible
- The Middle Eastern Vegetarian Cookbook — Salma Hage
- FALASTIN
- BAZAAR — Sabrina Ghayour — Vibrant Vegetarian Recipes
- ZAITOUN — Yasmin Khan
- tahini & turmeric — Vicky Cohen & Ruth Fox — 101 Middle Eastern Classics Made Irresistibly Vegan
- Vegan without Borders — Robertson
- BOTTOM of the POT — Persian Recipes and Stories — Naz Deravian
- THE KITCHEN without BORDERS — The Eat Offbeat Chefs
- OTTOLENGHI SIMPLE
- OTTOLENGHI — PLENTY
- OTTOLENGHI — FLAVOR
- Baking with Kim-Joy

Bottom shelf

- RACHAEL RAY'S BIG ORANGE BOOK
- RACHAEL RAY — 2, 4, 6, 8: Great Meals for Couples or Crowds
- RACHAEL RAY 30-Minute Meals
- RACHAEL RAY 50 — my year in meals
- ISA CHANDRA MOSKOWITZ — THE SUPERFUN TIMES Vegan Holiday Cookbook
- ina garten — modern comfort food
- Japanese Cooking with Manga
- ROBIN HA — Cook Korean! A Comic Book with Recipes
- LET'S MAKE RAMEN!
- Hello, Cupcake! — Karen Tack & Alan Richardson
- SOUP — Debra Mayhew
- THE Pepper Thai COOKBOOK — Pepper Teigen
- FORKS OVER KNIVES FAMILY — Alona Pulde, MD / Matthew Lederman, MD
- Cravings — HUNGRY FOR MORE — CHRISSY TEIGEN
- Cravings Made Vegan — HAUN & NADERER
- ANTONI IN THE KITCHEN — Antoni Porowski
- JESSICA SEINFELD — VEGAN AT TIMES
- SUPER TUSCAN — GABRIELE CORCOS and DEBI MAZAR
- EXTRA VIRGIN — Gabriele Corcos and Debi Mazar
- Chef's Vegan Comfort Cooking

CONTENTS

INTRODUCTION	1
WHAT IS COOKBOOK CLUB?	3
WHAT ARE PLANT-BASED FOODS?	5
TIPS FOR SUCCESS	6
THEME IDEAS	8
THE BASICS	14
APPETIZERS & SIDES	21
SOUPS	43
SALADS	63
MAINS	82
DESSERTS	119
GROCERY LIST	144
ACKNOWLEDGMENTS	146
INDEX	148

INTRODUCTION

I've amassed quite the collection of cookbooks over the years, but I never dreamt that I would ever write my own. This is going to sound a little crazy, but I used to hate cooking. I only really started learning how to cook out of necessity when I decided to become a vegetarian in 2007. Nowadays there are lots of plant-based options everywhere, but that was not the case back then. After a lot of trial and error, I realized that I actually really enjoyed experimenting with new dishes or better yet—changing some old favorites to vegetarian recipes so I could still eat them.

After receiving my bachelor's degree in Visual Arts Studies, I followed that with another bachelor's in Hospitality Management. After college, I ran/owned the first award winning vegetarian food truck in Denton, TX which I followed with a frozen food product in local grocery stores. In between all this I have taught cooking classes, worked as a kitchen manager at the first fully vegan college dining hall in the United States, and much more.

Let's just say—I've learned how to make some great recipes: sometimes through practice, sometimes through error, and sometimes through sheer luck.

Whether you are plant-based yourself or just interested in some new recipes for your Meatless Mondays, I appreciate you taking the time to look at this book! I hope I can convince anyone who looks through this to start a cookbook club of their own. It has been an amazing opportunity to bond with old friends and also to make new ones!

WHAT IS COOKBOOK CLUB?

Think of Cookbook Club as the coolest potluck you have ever been to.

Do you love the idea of having friends over to your house but didn't feel like you had a good occasion or a way to keep everyone entertained? Cookbook Club.

Have you ever had a dish you've been wanting to make but no one else in your family will eat it? Cookbook Club.

Want to test out a new recipe before you make it for a holiday dinner or big event? Cookbook Club.

Want to save money on groceries by taking home lots of amazing leftovers? Cookbook Club.

Want your friends to love you forever? Well, I can't promise Cookbook Club will do that, but it certainly won't hurt your chances either.

WHAT ARE PLANT-BASED FOODS?

THERE IS MUCH DEBATE OVER WHAT PLANT-BASED TECHNICALLY MEANS. FOR ME, PLANT-BASED DISHES ARE THOSE WHICH FOCUS ON PLANTS INSTEAD OF MEAT. PLANT-BASED RECIPES INCLUDE EITHER VEGETARIAN OR VEGAN DISHES. IN THE CATEGORY OF DESSERTS, MOST RECIPES ARE USUALLY PLANT-BASED ALREADY BUT THERE IS A DISTINCTION IN THAT PLANT-BASED DESSERTS DO NOT INCLUDE GELATIN.

VEGETARIAN DISHES OMIT ANIMAL PRODUCTS (INCLUDING GELATIN AND ANIMAL BROTHS) BUT STILL CONTAIN ANIMAL BY-PRODUCTS SUCH AS DAIRY, EGGS, AND HONEY.

VEGAN DISHES OMIT ALL ANIMAL PRODUCTS AND BY-PRODUCTS.

FOR THE PURPOSES OF THIS COOKBOOK, ALL RECIPES ARE VEGETARIAN. WITH THAT IN MIND, SOME OF THE RECIPES ARE ALSO VEGAN (V) AND/OR GLUTEN FREE (GF). THEY WILL BE LISTED AS SUCH AT THE END OF ANY RECIPE THAT APPLIES.

REMINDERS:

- MANY OF THE VEGETARIAN RECIPES IN THIS BOOK CAN BE MADE VEGAN BY SIMPLY SWAPPING THE DAIRY OUT WITH A NON-DAIRY ALTERNATIVE OF THE SAME ITEM.

- IF ANY BRAND NAMES ARE LISTED, YOU CAN OF COURSE SWAP THEM OUT WITH ANOTHER BRAND OF THE SAME ITEM.

- C: CUP
- OZ: OUNCE
- LB: POUND
- TSP: TEASPOON
- TBSP: TABLESPOON

let's get started!

TIPS FOR SUCCESS

SET UP A PRIVATE ONLINE GROUP WHERE YOU CAN SET UP AN EVENT PAGE EACH MONTH SO GUESTS CAN CHAT ABOUT WHAT THEY ARE BRINGING/ SHARE THEIR RECIPES.

COMPRISE A LIST OF FOOD ALLERGIES OF YOUR MOST FREQUENT GUESTS. CREATE A FORM THAT THEY CAN FILL OUT AND SET NEXT TO THEIR DISH (SEE PAGE 13 FOR EXAMPLE).

DO AN OCCASIONAL THEMED MONTH FOR FUN BUT THE LESS PARAMETERS ON WHAT PEOPLE CAN BRING, THE BETTER.

REMIND GUESTS TO BRING FOOD STORAGE CONTAINERS TO TAKE SOME OF THE LEFTOVERS HOME WITH THEM (AND SAVE UP YOUR TO-GO CONTAINERS FOR THOSE WHO FORGET).

SPREAD THE LOVE:

MAKE THE ENTRANCE "FEE" TO COOKBOOK CLUB A FEW CANS OF NON-PERISHABLE FOOD TO THEN DONATE TO A LOCAL FOOD PANTRY.

TIPS FOR SUCCESS

- JUST BECAUSE THERE ARE 10 GUESTS DOESN'T MEAN YOU NEED TO MAKE 10 FULL SERVINGS. THERE WILL BE SO MUCH FOOD TO TRY THAT EVERYONE ISN'T GOING TO WANT A LARGE SERVING.

- PAPER PLATES AND UTENSILS ARE YOUR FRIEND UNLESS YOU HAVE AN UNNATURAL LOVE OF WASHING LOTS OF DISHES. I SUGGEST THE COMPOSTABLE KIND TO TRY TO OFFSET THE WASTE.

- YOU CAN NEVER HAVE ENOUGH SERVING SPOONS. PEOPLE WILL INEVITABLY FORGET TO BRING THEIRS.

- WORRIED THERE WILL BE A LULL IN CONVERSATION? THERE ARE LOTS OF FUN FOOD-RELATED GAMES YOU CAN PURCHASE TO HAVE ON HAND TO BREAK THE ICE.

- COOKBOOK CLUB DOESN'T HAVE TO BE STRICTLY BASED OFF OF COOKBOOKS. YOU CAN USE A MIX OF COOKBOOKS, RECIPES OF YOUR OWN, AND RECIPES YOU FIND ONLINE.

murder mystery

cookbook club

tea party

cookbook club

pickle-themed cookbook club

spooky-themed

cookbook club

DISH:

Is this dish vegetarian/vegan?

Circle if it contains:

Walnuts
summer squash
zucchini
melons/cantaloupe/honeydew
pumpkin
avocado
banana
pineapple
sage
cream cheese
spinach
strawberries

THE BASICS

page 15: everyday salad dressing
page 15: citrus vinaigrette dressing
page 16: pickled onions
page 16: sumac onions
page 16: not-so-secret burger sauce
page 16: lemony pesto sauce
page 17: basic roasted vegetables
page 18: basic pizza dough
page 19: marinara sauce
page 19: alfredo sauce
page 19: artichoke & basil spread
page 20: cholula honey butter
page 20: taco seasoning

Learning these basic recipes gives you the building blocks you need for your plant-based foods journey. These are the recipes I usually like to have on hand to build a meal off of or to enhance a recipe.

everyday salad dressing

MAKES ABOUT 3/4 C.

Ingredients

1/2 c extra virgin olive oil
1/3 c lemon juice
1/2 tsp kosher salt
1/4 tsp ground black pepper

Directions

Whisk all ingredients together. Store in refrigerator until ready to use. (V, GF)

citrus vinaigrette dressing

MAKES 1 1/2 C. DRESSING

Ingredients

1 small shallot, finely minced
3/4 c extra virgin olive oil
1/4 c white wine vinegar
3 tbsp lemon juice
3 tbsp orange juice
1 lemon, zested
1/2 tsp kosher salt
1/4 tsp ground black pepper

Directions

Whisk all ingredients together. Store in refrigerator until ready to use. (V, GF)

pickled onions

MAKES ABOUT 2 C.

Ingredients

1 red onion, thinly sliced
4 tbsp rice vinegar
1/2 tsp kosher salt
juice and zest of 1 lime

Directions

Combine all ingredients in an airtight container with a lid. With the lid on, shake well to separate onion slices. Let sit in refrigerator for a minimum of an hour. The longer it sits, the better it will taste. Store in refrigerator until ready to use. (V, GF)

sumac onions

MAKES ABOUT 2 C.

Ingredients

1 yellow onion, thinly sliced
2 tbsp red wine vinegar
1 tbsp ground sumac
1/2 tsp kosher salt

Directions

Combine all ingredients in an airtight container with a lid. With the lid on, shake well to separate onion slices. Let sit in refrigerator for a minimum of an hour. The longer it sits, the better it will taste. Store in refrigerator until ready to use. (V, GF)

not-so-secret burger sauce

MAKES 3/4 C.

Ingredients

1/2 c mayonaisse
1/4 c ketchup
1 tbsp dijon mustard
1 tbsp relish
1 tbsp lemon juice
1 tbsp garlic powder
1/2 tsp kosher salt

Directions

Combine ingredients and refrigerate until ready to use. (GF)

lemony pesto sauce

MAKES 1/2 C.

Ingredients

1 c basil leaves
1/3 c parmesan cheese
1/4 c extra virgin olive oil
2 cloves garlic
2 tbsp pine nuts
juice and zest of one lemon
1/2 tsp kosher salt

Directions

Blend all ingredients together in a food processor until mostly smooth. (GF)

BASIC ROASTED VEGETABLES

THE KEY TO ROASTING VEGETABLES IS TO CUT THEM ALL INTO ABOUT THE SAME SIZE AND ALSO NOT TO CROWD YOUR BAKING SHEET. YOUR OPTIONS ARE ENDLESS WITH ROASTING VEGETABLES, HERE ARE SOME OF MY FAVORITES:

VEGETABLES

- bell peppers
- potatoes
- tomatoes
- onions
- zucchini/squash
- broccoli
- asparagus
- mushrooms

SEASONINGS

- kosher salt
- ground black pepper
- Italian seasoning
- oregano
- smoked paprika
- lemon pepper
- garlic powder
- onion powder

Preheat oven to 425 °F

Spread out vegetables in one layer on a parchment lined baking sheet. Evenly coat with olive oil and your chosen spices (always include salt). Bake 30-40 minutes or until vegetables are cooked through and browned, turning over once halfway through roasting.

NOW WHAT DO I DO WITH THESE ROASTED VEGETABLES?

- ADD TO PASTA
- SERVE OVER GREEK YOGURT
- ADD TO A WRAP WITH HUMMUS
- ADD ROASTED BEANS TO MAKE IT A COMPLETE MEAL
- SERVE TOPPED WITH AN EGG
- MAKE A ROASTED VEGETABLE SANDWICH

BASIC PIZZA DOUGH

WOW YOUR FRIENDS WITH YOUR OWN HOMEMADE PIZZA DOUGH. IT'S VERY SIMPLE TO MAKE AND THE BEST PART IS- IT CAN BE PREPPED AHEAD AND KEPT IN EITHER THE FRIDGE OR FREEZER TO MAKE LESS WORK ON THE DAY YOU WANT TO MAKE PIZZA. IT IS BEST FOR 3-5 DAYS STORED IN THE FRIDGE OR UP TO 3 MONTHS FROZEN.

INGREDIENTS

- 1 c + 1 tbsp hot water (about 110-115 degrees)
- 1 packet (2 1/4 tsp) active dry yeast
- 1 tsp granulated sugar
- 3 c all purpose flour
- 1 tsp kosher salt
- 1 tbsp extra virgin olive oil

DIRECTIONS

Put hot water in measuring cup. Immediately add yeast and sugar and whisk to combine. Let sit about 5-7 minutes until it mixture is frothy. (If your water is not at the correct temperature, the mixture won't froth and you'll need to do it again).

In a mixer, add the flour, salt, and olive oil. Slowly and the yeast mixture and mix using the dough hook attachment on 2 (low) speed for 30 seconds. Increase speed to 4 (medium) and mix for 3 minutes or until your dough ball forms. The mixture should not be too sticky and should form a ball. If the mixture is too dry, add water 1 tsp at a time until it comes together. If the mixture is too wet, add 1 tsp flour at a time until it comes together.

Coat a large bowl with oil and put your dough in. Cover and set aside in a dark place at room temperature for about an hour or until dough doubles in size.

Punch down the dough and roll it out onto a floured surface for use or cover tightly in saran wrap and set in refrigerator or freezer until you're ready to use it.

(V)

MAKES 1 LARGE OR 2 PERSONAL PIZZAS

marinara sauce

MAKES ABOUT 4 C.

Ingredients

4 tbsp extra virgin olive oil
1 small yellow onion, diced
2 garlic cloves, minced
1 celery stalk, diced
1 large carrot, diced
1 tsp kosher salt
1/4 tsp ground black pepper
1 tbsp dried oregano
1 tbsp dried thyme
1 tbsp dried basil
1/4 tsp red pepper flakes
1 bay leaf
1-28 oz can crushed tomatoes

Directions

In a large pan, heat the olive oil over medium heat. Add the onions and saute until translucent, about 10 minutes, stirring occasionally. Add the celery, carrots, garlic, salt, pepper, oregano, thyme, basil, and red pepper flakes. Saute until vegetables are soft, about 10 minutes, stirring occasionally. Add the bay leaf and crushed tomatoes. Simmer over low heat until the sauce thickens, about an hour. Add water or broth to sauce if it gets too thick.
(V, GF)

alfredo sauce

MAKES ABOUT 1 C.

Ingredients

1/4 c (4 tbsp) butter
3/4 c heavy whipping cream
1/2 tsp garlic powder
1/2 tsp Italian seasoning
1/4 tsp kosher salt
1/4 tsp ground black pepper
1/4 tsp ground nutmeg
3/4 c grated parmesan

Directions

Melt butter in a medium skillet over medium-low heat. Once melted, whisk in cream. Simmer for 2 minutes. Whisk in the remaining ingredients and cook 1 minute, stirring often, until cheese melts. (GF)

artichoke & basil spread

MAKES 1 C.

Ingredients

1-14 oz can artichoke hearts, drained
1/4 c fresh basil leaves
2 tbsp mayonnaise
1 tbsp lemon juice
1/2 tsp kosher salt
1/4 tsp ground black pepper

Directions

Blend ingredients together in a food processor until smooth. Refrigerate until ready to use. (GF)

cholula honey butter

MAKES 1/2 C.

Ingredients

1 stick (1/2 c) salted butter, softened
4 tbsp cholula hot sauce
2 tbsp honey

Directions

Combine ingredients and mix well. Pour onto plastic wrap and seal into a log shape. Refrigerate until ready to use. (GF)

taco seasoning

MAKES 6 TBSP

Ingredients

2 tbsp chili powder
1 tsp garlic pwder
1 tsp onion powder
1 tsp red pepper flakes
1 tsp dried oregano
2 tsp smoked paprika
1 tbsp ground cumin
2 tsp kosher salt
1 tsp ground black pepper

Directions

Combine ingredients together in a container. Store in pantry. (V, GF)

APPETIZERS & SIDES

page 23: potato poppers with two sauces
page 27: labneh bites
page 29: fried olives in yogurt sauce
page 31: joy's cranberry salsa
page 33: tomato-mayo toasts
page 35: yogurt stuffed eggplant
page 37: baked feta with roasted tomatoes & olives
page 39: pomegranate glazed eggplant
page 41: beet hummus and cottage cheese dip

potato poppers with two sauces

These were one of the most popular items on my food truck. Crispy on the outside, while soft and pillowy on the inside. Serve them with one (or both) of these sauces and they are sure to impress!

INGREDIENTS

2 1/2 c instant dried mashed potato flakes
2 1/2 c water
1/4 large yellow onion, minced
3/4 c all purpose flour
2 tsp baking powder
1 tbsp cornstarch
1 tbsp zaatar
1 tbsp kosher salt
1/4 tsp ground black pepper
2 eggs
1/2 c fresh, chopped parsley; plus more for garnish
48 oz vegetable oil, for frying
feta & cream cheese and/or beet yogurt sauces, for garnish

DIRECTIONS

Bring the 2 1/2 c water to a boil, then set aside to cool for about 3 minutes.

In a large heatproof bowl, carefully add the hot water to the potato flakes and mix well.

Add in the minced onion, flour, baking powder, cornstarch, zaatar, salt, and pepper. Mix to combine and set aside for 10 minutes to cool down a bit.

Add in the eggs and 1/2 c parsley, then mix together one last time.

Heat the vegetable oil in a deep, heavy pot over medium heat to about 350-375 °F.

Once you're ready, use a tiny scoop to gently add the batter to the hot frying oil-BE VERY CAREFUL NOT TO HAVE HOT OIL POP BACK UP AT YOU! Each scoop should be about 2 tbsp worth of the batter.

Fry in batches for about 6-8 minutes per batch, until golden brown all around—stirring occasionally to make sure they don't stick together.

Remove from fryer oil and lay on a paper-towel lined tray to absorb some of the excess oil before serving.

Top with one (or both) sauces and a sprinkle of parsley.

MAKES ABOUT 32 POPPERS

feta & cream cheese sauce

INGREDIENTS

8 oz cream cheese, softened
3/4 c water, or more as needed
1 tbsp extra virgin olive oil
1/2 c feta cheese
1 tbsp lemon juice
small handful fresh mint, stems removed
small handful fresh dill, stems removed
1/4 tsp ground black pepper

DIRECTIONS

In a food processor, blend all the ingredients together until smooth. Add more water as desired to thin the sauce out a bit.

Stays good in the refrigerator for about a week. This sauce is also great as a vegetable dip or sandwich spread.

(GF)

a few notes on this recipe

- The best feta for this is french feta (in brine). You may need to adjust the water ratio if using dry, crumbled feta.
- In a pinch, you can use dried mint and dill instead of fresh.

MAKES ABOUT 2 1/2C. SAUCE

beet yogurt sauce

INGREDIENTS

1 1/2 c (12 oz) full-fat Greek yogurt
1 medium red beet, washed and trimmed
2 tsp extra virgin olive oil
1 tsp kosher salt
1/4 tsp ground black pepper

DIRECTIONS

Preheat oven to 450 °F.

Bake beet in foil for about 45 minutes or until cooked through. Let it cool enough to handle, then peel and roughly chop.

Place chopped beets in a food processor, along with the yogurt, olive oil, salt, and pepper. Blend until smooth (you can add a little water if you want a thinner consistency).

Stays good in the refrigerator for about a week. This sauce is also great as a vegetable dip or sandwich spread.

WANT A QUICKER VERSION OF THIS SAUCE?

Swap the roasted beet with a 3/4 drained can of beets (not the pickled kind).

(GF)

BEHOLD, THE GREAT FOOD TRUCK BEET SAUCE MASSACRE OF 2017. LEARN YOUR LESSON FROM ME, KIDS: MAKE SURE THE LIDS ON YOUR BOTTLES ARE ALWAYS SECURE!

MAKES ABOUT 1 ½ C. SAUCE

labneh bites

Labneh is a soft Middle Eastern cheese made from strained yogurt. You can buy it in specialty stores but it is infinitely better when you make it yourself. These bites are super easy to make but do require a little forethought as they take a little bit of babysitting during the straining process. Serve them with a drizzle of olive oil and whatever seasoning you choose. The options are endless.

INGREDIENTS

1- 32 oz container full-fat Greek yogurt
1/2 tsp kosher salt
good quality extra virgin olive oil, for storage
spices for serving or coating (ex: zaatar, red pepper flakes, dried mint, etc)

cheesecloth, for straining

DIRECTIONS

Place a colander into a larger bowl to catch liquids. Place a large piece of cheesecloth in the colander and pour in the yogurt. Wrap the cheesecloth over the top of the yogurt and then fit a plate on top.

Top your plate with something heavy, like a jar or two of salsa, and refrigerate at least 12 hours (24 if possible). Transfer the drained yogurt to a bowl and mix in the salt.

Form the yogurt into walnut sized balls (it will still be fairly wet at this point)

Lay a layer of paper towel in a dish and set labneh balls on top about 1/2" apart from each other. Top with another layer of paper towel and let them dry out another 12-24 hours in the refrigerator. (You will want to change the paper towels out a few times throughout as they soak up the liquid).

Reshape the balls into firmer circles and serve drizzled with olive oil and sprinkled with seasonings (or coat completely in seasoning).

If you won't be serving these immediately, store the plain yogurt balls in a container with enough olive oil to cover in the refrigerator. Set out for about 20 minutes before serving.

(GF)

MAKES 10-12 BITES

fried olives in yogurt sauce

There is something about a hot, crunchy olive mixed with a cool, creamy yogurt sauce that makes this recipe vanish very quickly. Adding the herb drizzle to the yogurt sauce adds some extra flavor but you can add any flavorings you want. Hot sauce, pesto, or even some pasta sauce are also great to mix in.

INGREDIENTS

1 c cilantro, chopped
1/2 c parsley, chopped
1/4 c mint, chopped
3 tbsp extra virgin olive oil
1 tsp kosher salt, divided

3/4 c bread crumbs
6 tbsp all purpose flour
2 eggs, beaten
1 c pitted caselvetrano olives, drained and patted dry
vegetable oil, for frying

1 c full-fat Greek yogurt

DIRECTIONS

In a food processor, combine the cilantro, parsley, mint, olive oil, and 1/2 tsp of the salt and blend until combined into a semi-thick paste. Set aside.

Set up your coating station by placing three bowls side by side. Fill one with the bread crumbs, one with the flour, and one with the beaten eggs.

Before you start coating the olives, heat about 2" of the vegetable oil in a cast iron skillet over medium heat.

While the oil is heating up, take one of the olives and dip it in the flour, then the egg, then the bread crumbs-making sure to coat well at each step. Place on a plate and repeat with remaining olives.

Once the oil is hot, carefully add in about half of the coated olives. Cook 1-2 minutes or until golden-brown, carefully turning over occasionally to make sure they brown all around. Remove and set aside. Repeat with other half of olives and add to reserved fried olives.

In a small bowl, mix together the yogurt with the remaining 1/2 tsp of salt, then spread into a shallow serving bowl, leaving a well in the center. Spread the herb drizzle over the yogurt and place the fried olives in the center to serve.

SERVES 4

joy's cranberry salsa

My sister-in-law introduced this recipe at one of our holiday get-togethers and it has been requested many times since then. The bright flavor and color of the cranberry make this festive dish a hit for any party.

INGREDIENTS

10 oz bag fresh cranberries
1/4 c finely diced white onion
1 small jalapeno, minced (*see note)
1/4 c chopped cilantro
1 tbsp sugar, or to taste
1 tbsp lime juice, or to taste
1/2 tsp kosher salt, or to taste
tortilla chips, to serve

DIRECTIONS

In a food processor, pulse cranberries to a small but rough chop. Pour into a bowl and combine with remaining ingredients. Adjust seasonings as desired. Allow to sit in fridge for at least an hour before serving to meld flavors together.

Serve with tortilla chips (this recipe is also great with a side of goat cheese).

*note on the jalapeno: you can remove the seeds from the jalapeno before chopping for a less spicy flavor.

(V, GF)

SERVES 4-6

tomato-mayo toasts

I already know what you are thinking: What is so special about a tomato sandwich? I am here to tell you that there is something about the perfect combination of bread, mayonnaise, tomatoes, and seasonings that makes this a meal I literally dream about. Easily one of my top favorite sandwiches. The key is to get the nicest version of all the ingredients that you can.

INGREDIENTS

6 slices thickly cut sourdough bread
12 tbsp mayonnaise, divided
approx. 2 large or 4 medium tomatoes, sliced
kosher salt and ground black pepper, to taste

DIRECTIONS

Preheat oven to 350 °F.

Place sliced bread on a baking sheet and bake for about 5 minutes or until toasted. Set aside for about 5 minutes to cool off a bit.

Spread 2 tbsp of mayo on each toast. Top with sliced tomatoes and a sprinkle of salt and pepper.

MAKES ABOUT 6 TOASTS

yogurt stuffed eggplant

Not only is this a tasty dish- but it's a real stunner as well. Roasting any vegetable elevates the flavors and this recipe really showcases that. Remember when I said that cookbook club is a great excuse to cook meals your family doesn't like? My husband is not an eggplant fan, so this is something I like to make when people are over so lots of people can try it.

INGREDIENTS

2 large eggplants
9 tbsp extra virgin olive oil, divided
4 tsp thyme leaves, divided
2 tsp kosher salt, divided
1/4 tsp ground black pepper
1 tsp zaatar seasoning
1/2 c heavy cream
1/2 c full-fat Greek yogurt
1 clove garlic, minced
pomegranate seeds, for garnish

DIRECTIONS

Preheat oven to 400 °F.

Cut each eggplant in half lengthwise (including the stalks). Then, for each eggplant half, carefully cut a few parallel lines facing one way (don't pierce all the way through) and then do the same in the opposite direction to create a cross hatch pattern.

Place the eggplant halves, cut side up, on a parchment lined baking sheet. Brush them evenly with 6 tbsp of the olive oil (make sure to use all the oil as the eggplant will soak it all in). Sprinkle with 1 tsp of the salt, 1/4 tsp pepper, and 2 tsp of the thyme leaves. Roast for about 40 minutes, or until eggplant is fully cooked through and browned. Remove from the oven and set aside to cool for 10 minutes.

While the eggplants are roasting in the oven, make the yogurt sauce by combining the cream, yogurt, minced garlic, 1 tbsp of the olive oil, and 1 tsp of salt.

Once eggplants have cooled, place on your serving tray and spoon yogurt sauce on top. Sprinkle the zaatar and 2 remaining tsp of thyme leaves over top. Drizzle 1 tbsp of the olive oil over them and garnish with pomegranate seeds.

(GF)

SERVES 4

baked feta with roasted tomatoes, peppers & olives

This is comfort food at it's finest. The warm cheese just melts onto the bread. The sharp flavor of the cheese compliments the sweet peppers and tomatoes to create the perfect bite.

INGREDIENTS

1 c cherry tomatoes, halved
1 red bell pepper, chopped
1/2 c caselvetrano olives
2 tsp dried oregano
1/2 tsp kosher salt
1/4 tsp ground black pepper
8 oz feta cheese block, cut in half
2 tbsp extra virgin olive oil
chopped parsley, for garnish
Bread or crackers, for serving

DIRECTIONS

Preheat oven to 400 °F.

In a bowl, combine the chopped tomatoes, chopped bell pepper, and olives with the oregano, salt, and pepper. Mix to combine.

Place 2 pieces of feta in the center of an ovenproof dish, about an inch apart from each other. Top with the tomato mixture and bake until tomatoes are roasted, about 20-25 minutes. Remove from oven. Drizzle with the olive oil and garnish with parsley.

Serve warm with bread or crackers.

SERVES 6-8

pomegranate glazed eggplant

This dish is deceptively easy to make and makes a great side dish. It's also great as a meal alongside some rice. The ingredient that does all the work here is the pomegranate molasses-a staple in Middle Eastern cooking.

INGREDIENTS

2 large eggplants, half peeled
1/3 c extra virgin olive oil
1/3 c pomegranate molasses
sprinkle of kosher salt
pomegranate seeds, for garnish

DIRECTIONS

Preheat your oven to broil.

Line a sheet pan with parchment paper.

In a bowl, whisk together the oil and molasses.

Cut off the stem of the eggplant and a little off the bottom, then peel half of the skin off with a peeler, leaving a little bit on. Cut the eggplant in half lengthwise and then cut those further in half crosswise. This should leave you with 4 big pieces per eggplant. Cut each piece into 4 wedge shaped pieces. This should leave you with about 32 wedges. Coat completely in olive oil mixture and lay on prepared baking sheet. Brush on any remaining oil mixture evenly over eggplant. Sprinkle with salt.

Broil 8 minutes on one side, then flip and cook 5 more minutes. Remove from oven and allow to cool a few minutes before serving.

Serve topped with pomegranate seeds. Great served along with yogurt or labneh bites from page 27.

(V, GF)

SERVES 6-8

beet hummus

Have you ever seen such a pretty dip? The roasted beets give this dish an amazing flavor and are also the key to that pretty pink hue. Elevate your hummus game and try this version next time you make it.

INGREDIENTS

1 medium red beet, washed and trimmed
1- 15 oz can chickpeas, rinsed and drained
3 tbsp tahini
3 tbsp lemon juice
2 tbsp extra virgin olive oil, plus more for garnish
1 tbsp garlic powder
1 tsp kosher salt
1/2 tsp ground cumin
1/4 tsp ground black pepper
chopped parsley, for garnish

DIRECTIONS

Preheat oven to 450 °F.

Bake beet in foil for about 45 minutes or until cooked through. Let it cool enough to handle, then peel and roughly chop.

Place chopped beets in a food processor, along with the chickpeas (reserving a few for your garnish), tahini, lemon juice, 2 tbsp olive oil, garlic powder, salt, cumin, and pepper. Blend to combine. If hummus is too thick, thin it out by adding 1 tbsp of water at a time until you reach desired consistency.

Serve in a bowl garnished with a drizzle of olive oil and a sprinkle of the reserved chickpeas and chopped parsley.

WANT A QUICKER VERSION OF THIS HUMMUS?

Swap the roasted beet with a 3/4 drained can of beets (not the pickled kind).

(V, GF)

SERVES 4-6

cottage cheese dip

This dip packs the protein and the flavor! Blending the cottage cheese gives it a smooth, silky texture that rivals any other cheese dip. It's also great as a sandwich spread!

INGREDIENTS

- 1 c full-fat cottage cheese
- 2 tbsp lemon juice
- 1 tbsp tahini
- 1 tbsp extra virgin olive oil
- 1 tsp garlic powder
- 1 tsp onion powder
- 1/2 tsp kosher salt
- 1/4 tsp ground black pepper
- smoked paprika and chopped fresh parsley, for garnish
- vegetables or crackers, for serving

DIRECTIONS

In a food processor, blend together the cottage cheese, lemon juice, tahini, olive oil, and seasonings. If dip is too thick, thin it out by adding 1 tbsp of water at a time until you reach desired consistency.

When ready to serve, garnish with a sprinkle of smoked paprika and chopped parsley.

Serve alongside crackers or vegetables for dipping.

(GF)

SERVES 4-6

SOUPS

page 45: broccoli & feta soup
page 47: chickpea noodle soup
page 49: ash reshteh
page 51: white bean and kale soup
page 53: coconut soup with tofu
page 55: tomato soup with grilled cheese croutons
page 59: minestrone soup with tortellini
page 61: seattle chowder

broccoli & feta soup

In addition to the cottage cheese fan club, I am also a member of the soup all year round fan club. Luckily my schedule allows me to be members of both. This is one of those soups that is amazing served both hot or cold.

INGREDIENTS

1 lb broccoli, roughly chopped

4 c vegetable broth

2 c water

3 cloves garlic, minced

1 tsp kosher salt, or to taste

1/4 tsp pepper, or to taste

1/2 c small shell pasta such as orzo

8 tbsp feta cheese, crumbled

lemon juice, for garnish

DIRECTIONS

Roughly chop the broccoli, including stems, and place in a pot. Add the garlic, broth, water, salt, and pepper. Bring to a boil, then reduce to a simmer over medium heat. Cover the pot and cook for 30 minutes or until broccoli has softened.

Gently mash broccoli with a masher a few times to break down the broccoli. Add pasta and continue to cook for 10 more minutes or until pasta is cooked through, stirring occasionally.

Remove the soup from the burner and stir in the feta cheese.

Ladle soup into bowls and top with a squeeze of lemon juice.

SERVES 4

chickpea noodle soup

This soup is just as hearty as the one your mom would make you when you were sick-but now you don't even have to call off work to have it. (I wont tell anyone if you do though-your secret is safe with me). I personally love to add a shocking amount of lemon juice to this soup at the end but that part is totally up to you.

INGREDIENTS

1 tbsp. extra virgin olive oil

1 yellow onion, diced

2 carrots, thinly sliced

3 celery stalks, sliced

3 garlic cloves, minced

1 tsp dried thyme

6 c vegetable broth

1 c water

1- 15 oz can chickpeas, rinsed and drained

1 bay leaf

1 c orzo or other small noodle

1 tsp kosher salt, or to taste

1 tsp ground black pepper, or to taste

1/4 c lemon juice, or to taste

lemon slices, for garnish

DIRECTIONS

Heat the olive oil over medium heat. Add the onions, carrots, celery, and garlic. Cook for 5 minutes or until vegetables have softened.

Add the thyme, salt, pepper, bay leaf, and stir together. Add the broth and water and bring to a boil.

Add the chickpeas and orzo. Reduce heat to medium-low and simmer 10 more minutes or until orzo is cooked through.

Remove from heat and stir in lemon juice.

Ladle into bowls and garnish with lemon slices.

(V)

SERVES 4-6

ash reshteh

This is a classic Iranian beans, greens, and noodle soup. There are specific noodles you can buy at Middle Eastern markets (or online) for it but you can substitute with a linguine or any other long noodle that can stand up to cooking for a while without getting mushy.

INGREDIENTS

2 tbsp extra virgin olive oil
1 yellow onion, chopped
2 tsp salt
1 tsp ground black pepper
1 tbsp turmeric
1/3 c uncooked brown lentils
6 c vegetable broth
2 c water
10 oz spinach, chopped
1 bunch cilantro, chopped
1 bunch parsley, chopped
10 green onions, chopped
1-15 oz can chickpeas, rinsed and drained
1-15 oz can kidney beans, rinsed and drained
1 tbsp all purpose flour
6 oz reshteh noodles, broken into 1" pieces
sour cream (optional), to garnish

DIRECTIONS

Heat the olive oil to a large pot over medium heat. Add onion, salt, pepper, and turmeric. Saute about 8 minutes or until onions are browned and very soft.

Add the lentils and saute for one minute. Add the broth and water. Bring to a boil and cook for 5 minutes. Add spinach, cilantro, parsley, green onions, chickpea and kidney beans, and broken noodles. Mix well to combine.

In a small bowl, make a slurry by mixing 1 tbsp. flour with 2 tbsp. cold water. Add slurry to the soup and cook 5 more minutes, then reduce to a simmer on medium-low heat. Cook 30 more minutes, stirring occasionally.

Ladle into bowls and top with a dollop of sour cream, if desired.

SERVES 4-6

white bean and kale soup

One New Year's eve, our game night group decided all our families would drive out to the country and share a house together for the long weekend. Every family was in charge of bringing some of the food for everyone and this was one of the dishes I brought. It was a hit with everyone—even picky children!

INGREDIENTS

1 yellow onion, finely chopped
2 tbsp extra virgin olive oil
1 tsp kosher salt
1/4 tsp ground black pepper
4 garlic cloves, minced
2 large carrots, peeled and chopped
1 stalk celery, diced
2 tbsp tomato paste
2-15 oz cans cannelini beans, rinsed and drained
1 tsp Italian seasoning
3 tsp fresh (or 1 tsp dried) thyme
3 tsp fresh (or 1 tsp dried) oregano
1 bay leaves
6 c vegetable broth
1 small bunch kale, chopped (stems removed)
3 oz small noodles (ex: orzo)
warm bread, for serving

DIRECTIONS

Heat the olive oil in a dutch oven over medium heat. Add the chopped onion, salt, and pepper. Saute for 7 minutes, stirring occasionally, until onions start to slightly brown. add in the garlic, carrots, and celery. Saute 10 more minutes, stirring occasionally, until vegetables have softened.

Add the tomato paste and stir to coat all the vegetables. Cook for one minute. Add in the beans, all the seasonings, the bay leaf, and the broth. Bring to a boil over high heat, then cover and simmer for 15 minutes over medium heat. Add the in the chopped kale and noodles and simmer until noodles are cooked through, stirring occasionally, about 9-10 minutes.

Serve with warm bread (don't forget to pull out they bay leaf).

SERVES 6

coconut soup with tofu

This broth is magical. The soup comes together quickly, and the addition of the tofu makes it filling. If you wanted to make it a little extra filling, rice noodles are a great addition as well.

INGREDIENTS

6 c vegetable broth
1- 13.5 oz can full-fat coconut milk
1- 14 oz package extra firm tofu, chopped into small squares
2 leeks, thinly sliced and rinsed well
1- 0.5 oz package basil, cut thin (chiffonade); reserve a little for garnish
1 tbsp sesame oil
1 tbsp rice vinegar
1 tbsp lemon juice
1/2 tsp kosher salt
1/4 tsp ground black pepper

DIRECTIONS

In a large pot, bring broth and coconut milk to a boil over high heat, stirring often with a whisk to dissolve all the coconut milk solids. Once the broth is boiling, reduce it to a simmer over medium heat.

Carefully add the leeks and cook 5-7 minutes or until they begin to soften. Add the sesame oil, vinegar, lemon juice, and tofu (add tofu in a little at a time so the hot broth doesn't splash into your face). Cook 5 more minutes, stirring occasionally.

Add most of the basil and cook 5 more minutes. Taste the soup and add more seasonings, as desired.

Ladle into bowls and garnish with more basil.

(V, GF)

SERVES 4

tomato soup with grilled cheese croutons

Why would you ever go back to regular croutons after you've had this kind? This is a different take on a classic pairing. Roasting the vegetables makes this taste so much better than something you would get out of a can.

INGREDIENTS

for soup:

one head of garlic

6 medium tomatoes, cored and chopped

1 red bell pepper, seeded and chopped

4 tbsp extra virgin olive oil, divided

2 tsp kosher salt

2 tbsp salted butter

1 yellow onion, diced

2 tbsp chopped fresh basil, plus more for garnish

2 tbsp Italian seasoning

6 oz Italian-style tomato paste

2 c vegetable broth

1 tbsp sugar

1/4 tsp ground black pepper

1 c heavy cream

*ingredients continue on next page

DIRECTIONS

Preheat oven to 425 °F.

Cut off the top of the head of garlic (these scraps would be great for your homemade broth-see page 57). Place in a piece of foil and drizzle 1 tbsp of the olive oil on top. Firmly close foil around the garlic and roast in oven for 20 minutes.

In the meantime, chop tomatoes and bell pepper into large chunks. Place them on a rimmed baking sheet lined with parchment paper. Coat with 2 tbsp of the olive oil and 2 tsp salt. Once garlic has been roasting in the oven for 20 minutes, use oven mitts to carefully remove it from the oven and place the foil wrapped garlic on your baking sheet along with the tomatoes and peppers. Place this in the oven and roast another 20 minutes.

After the tomato mixture has been roasting for 20 minutes, set your oven temperature to broil (keeping baking sheet in oven) and broil for 7-8 minutes or until tops of tomato mixture start to char. Turn off oven and remove baking sheet. Set aside to cool.

*recipe continues on next page

MAKES 6-8 SERVINGS SOUP

tomato soup with grilled cheese croutons (continued)

INGREDIENTS

for each grilled cheese serving:

2 slices bread

2 oz muenster cheese, shredded

1 oz cheddar cheese, shredded

1 tbsp unsalted butter, melted

DIRECTIONS

While tomato/garlic mixture is cooling off, set a dutch oven or large pot on stovetop over medium heat. Add 2 tbsp butter and 1 tbsp of the olive oil. Once butter has melted, add the chopped onion and saute for 8-10 minutes, stirring occasionally, until onion is mostly softened.

Add the 2 tbsp chopped basil, italian seasoning, and tomato paste. Cook 2 more minutes, stirring frequently. Add the roasted tomatoes and peppers (and the reserved juices from the pan). Make sure garlic is cool enough to handle, then squeeze the roasted garlic out of the skin and into the soup mixture (the leftover roasted garlic skins would also be great for your freezer broth). Cook 2 more minutes then reduce heat to low. Add the broth, sugar, pepper, and heavy cream. Stir to combine. Remove pot from heat and blend to desired texture using an immersion blender, then set back on low heat while you prepare the grilled cheese croutons, adjusting seasonings if desired.

Assemble as many grilled cheeses as needed for how many you will be serving. For each sandwich, coat each side with half of the butter and cook on stovetop 3-4 minutes per side over medium heat, until bread is toasted and cheese is melted. Place on cutting board and cut into crouton squares with a sharp knife.

Ladle soup into bowls and top with grilled cheese croutons and basil, to garnish.

a "souper" tip:

Want to save the planet and some money as well? Keep a container in your freezer, and whenever you have some soup-worthy scraps or veggies that are a bit past their prime (see list) add them in there. Once your container is full- make this vegetable broth! This reduces your trash and saves you a trip to the grocery store. Your soup discards can be put in the compost pile once you're done with them.

DIRECTIONS

Add your frozen scraps to a large pot, then enough water to cover about 3/4 of your scraps. Add a bay leaf (optional), and whatever dried spices you would like.

Bring broth to a boil, then reduce heat to a simmer on medium high and cook for an hour to allow the flavors to meld. At this point, add 2 tsp of salt (or to taste) as well as 1 tsp baking soda*. (Be careful to leave room in the pot as the addition of the baking soda will make it bubble for about a minute). Take the pot off the heat and set aside.

Place a large strainer inside a large, heatproof bowl. Carefully ladle in broth to separate the solids and liquids (discard solids). Allow broth to cool to room temperature before storing (about 2 hours).

*It's best to add your salt at the end of making broth because as the liquid reduces during cooking, the flavors concentrate, which could lead to an overly salty broth. The addition of the baking soda neutralizes the acidity and creates a more balanced flavor.

***My favorite scraps for this are celery, tomatoes, onions, carrots, mushrooms, peppers, herbs, and garlic.

***Broth will stay good in the fridge for a few days or in the freezer for about 6 months.

***Other great add-ons at the time of cooking would be the last bits of your jarred salsa and/or pasta sauce. It will add an extra layer to the flavor of your broth.

minestrone soup with tortellini

There is a certain restaurant that I still love to frequent because of their unlimited salad and minestrone soup. Adding the tortellini in place of the more traditional small shell pasta makes this soup more filling.

INGREDIENTS

2 tbsp extra virgin olive oil

1 small onion, diced

1 small zucchini, diced

1 small squash, diced

2 carrots, diced

2 celery stalks, sliced

1 tsp kosher salt

1/4 tsp ground black pepper

4 garlic cloves, minced

4 tbsp tomato paste

2 tsp Italian seasoning

7 c vegetable broth

1 bay leaf

1-28 oz can diced tomatoes, undrained

1-15 oz can each of kidney and cannelini beans, rinsed and drained

4 c (about 6 oz) baby spinach

1-9 oz package cheese tortellini

DIRECTIONS

Heat the olive oil in a large pot over medium heat, then add the onion, zucchini, squash, carrots, celery, salt, and pepper. Cook 15 minutes, stirring occasionally, until vegetables begin to soften.

Add garlic and cook an additional 2-3 minutes to soften.

Add the tomato paste and Italian seasoning and cook an additional minute, stirring to coat the vegetables. Add the broth, bay leaf, diced tomatoes and their juices, kidney beans, and cannelini beans. Stir to combine and bring soup to a boil over high heat, then reduce to medium-low and simmer for 15 minutes.

Increase heat to medium and stir in the spinach and the tortellini. Cook for 5 minutes or until pasta is cooked through.

Remove bay leaf and ladle into bowls.

SERVES 6-8

seattle chowder

On a recent trip to Seattle, I tried the most amazing vegan chowder I've ever had in my life. This is my homage to it. The lime juice in the coconut broth is the magic key to this amazing chowder.

INGREDIENTS

4 tbsp extra virgin olive oil, divided

6 oz baby bella mushrooms, diced small

2 stalks celery, thinly sliced

1 medium yellow onion, diced small

1 small leek (white and light green parts), thinly sliced

1 tsp kosher salt

1/4 tsp ground black pepper

4 cloves garlic, minced

1/4 c all purpose flour

4 c vegetable broth

1- 13.5 oz can full-fat coconut milk

3/4 lb golden potatoes, diced

1 tbsp curry powder

1 bay leaf

1 tsp dried thyme

1 tsp old bay seasoning

1- 14oz (4g) package roasted seaweed sheets

3/4 c frozen corn kernels

1/3 c lime juice (from about 2 limes)

oyster crackers, chives, and lime wedges; for garnish

*directions on next page

SERVES 6

seattle chowder (continued)

DIRECTIONS

Heat 2 tbsp of the olive oil over medium heat in a dutch oven. Add mushrooms in a single layer and toss to coat in the oil. Saute 8 minutes or until mushrooms are browned, stirring occasionally.

Remove the mushrooms and set aside in a bowl. Add in the remaining 2 tbsp of the olive oil and add the celery, onion, leeks (see note at bottom of page), salt, and pepper. Cook for about 5 minutes, stirring occasionally, until onions have softened. Add the garlic and flour. Stir to coat all the mixture in the flour and allow to cook for 2 more minutes, stirring occasionally.

Add the reserved mushrooms, broth, coconut milk, potatoes, curry powder, bay leaf, thyme, and old bay seasoning. Crumble in the package of seaweed and stir to combine. Bring to a boil over high heat, then reduce to a simmer over medium heat. Gently stir in the corn.

Allow mixture to simmer until potatoes have softened, 20-25 minutes, stirring occasionally.

Remove pot from the heat and stir in the lime juice. Remove bay leaf and ladle into bowls. Garnish with crackers, chives, and lime wedges.

(V)

***A note about leeks: make sure you thoroughly clean your leeks before adding them to the chowder. Once they are sliced, put them in a bowl full of water and move them around a bit with your hands to loosen the dirt out of the layers.

SALADS

page 65: maman's pasta salad
page 67: tabbouli
page 69: kale and fruit salad
page 71: cheeseburger salad
page 73: salad shirazi
page 75: caesar salad with fried artichokes
page 77: watermelon & feta salad
page 79: mediterranean rice salad
page 81: celebration salad

maman's pasta salad

I come from a family of pickle lovers. This pasta salad is no exception. It does beg the question though—is this a salad or a side dish? After much debate, I have put it in this salad section—but I'm not 100% secure in my stance on that.

INGREDIENTS

- 1-12 oz box rainbow pasta
- 1 c frozen peas
- 1 pint multicolor cherry tomatoes, halved
- 10 pickles, diced -or to taste
- 4 stalks celery, chopped small
- 1 c mayonaisse
- 2 tbsp lemon juice
- 2 tbsp extra virgin olive oil
- 1 tsp kosher salt
- 1 tbsp lemon pepper
- 1 tbsp garlic powder

DIRECTIONS

Cook pasta in salted, boiling water according to package instructions. About 2 minutes before pasta is done, carefully add frozen peas so they can cook through. Once pasta and peas are ready, drain and then rinse under cool water. Make sure you drain off as much water as possible once pasta has cooled off.

Add your chopped tomatoes, pickles, and celery to the drained pasta and mix well. Add the mayonnaise, lemon juice, olive oil, salt, lemon pepper, and garlic powder. Mix gently to combine. Taste and adjust seasonings if desired.

SERVES 4-6

tabbouli

Another food truck favorite—tabbouli is another Middle Eastern staple. It's a bulgur wheat salad that actually tastes even better the next day after the flavors have really had a chance to meld. It's great for meal prepping as it's a very hearty salad that stands up to sitting in the fridge for a few days.

INGREDIENTS

3 c #3 bulgur wheat grains (this is the coarsest type)
3 c boiling water
1 tbsp + 1 tsp salt, divided
1 c lemon juice
1/2 c extra virgin olive oil
1 english cucumber, partially peeled and finely diced
5 roma tomatoes, finely diced
1 bunch parsley, minced
1 bunch cilantro, minced
1 large handful fresh mint leaves, minced
1 small red onion, finely diced
3 garlic cloves, minced
1/2 tsp ground black pepper

DIRECTIONS

Place bulgur in a large heatproof bowl and top with boiling water and 1 tbsp. salt. Mix well and set aside 30-45 min. or until bulgur is cooked through, stirring occasionally.

Meanwhile, combine the chopped cucumber, tomatoes, parsley, cilantro, mint, onion, and garlic.

Once the bulgur is cooked through- drain any excess liquid, if needed. Add to bowl with vegetables and mix well to combine.

Add the remaining 1 tsp salt, 1 c lemon juice, 1/2 c olive oil, and 1/2 tsp pepper. Taste and readjust seasonings if desired.

Refrigerate at least 1 hour before serving. Mix well before serving.

(V)

SERVES 8

kale and fruit salad

I can not tell you the amount of times I have had requests for the recipe for this salad. The key is to really massage the kale for a few minutes to soften it. It's very versatile-literally any fruit you have on hand tastes great in it.

INGREDIENTS

1 bunch kale, stalks removed, chopped
1 lemon, juiced (2-3 tbsp worth)
1/4 c extra virgin olive oil
1/2 tsp kosher salt
1/4 tsp ground black pepper
2 tsp honey
assorted fruit, chopped

Pro tip: save any juices from cutting your fruit and add them to the dressing to amplify the taste.

DIRECTIONS

In a large serving bowl, add the chopped kale, salt, pepper, and about half the lemon juice and olives oil. Massage for 2-3 minutes or until the kale starts to soften and wilt.

Add in the rest of the olive oil and lemon juice, as well as the honey. Add the chopped fruit and stir to combine. Re-season to taste.

(GF)

SERVES 4

cheeseburger salad

You heard me. Cheeseburger. Salad.

This recipe went viral a while back and this is my vegetarian take on it. I could literally inhale a vat of this if you let me.

INGREDIENTS

1 small head iceberg lettuce, shredded

1-10 oz package ground beef-style crumbles

1 c shredded cheddar cheese

2 pickles, finely diced

4 tbsp finely chopped white onion

2 tbsp mayonaisse

1 tbsp ketchup

1 tbsp dijon mustard

1 tsp pickle juice

1/2 tsp onion powder

1/2 tsp dried dill or 2 tbsp chopped fresh dill

sesame seeds, to garnish

DIRECTIONS

Cook the beef crumbles according to package instructions.

Meanwhile, make the sauce in large bowl by whisking together the mayo, ketchup, mustard, pickle juice, onion powder and dill.

Add the shredded lettuce, pickles, and onions to the bowl and combine well.

Add the cheddar and the cooked beef crumbles. Stir again to combine everything.

Garnish with sesame seeds.

SERVES 4-6

baba's shirazi salad

This is an Iranian favorite and no one makes it better than my dad. If you are as patient as he is, you can cut everything into teeny tiny pieces which is visually stunning. I lack his patience, so I do a regular small dice. No matter the shape, it all tastes great!

INGREDIENTS

6 roma tomatoes, diced

1 english cucumber, half peeled; diced (or 6 persian cucumbers)

1/2 c finely diced white onion

4 tbsp extra virgin olive oil

1/2 c lemon juice-or to taste

3 tbsp. dried mint (or use minced, fresh mint)

1 tsp kosher salt- or to taste

1/2 tsp ground black pepper

DIRECTIONS

Combine the chopped tomato, cucumber, and onion in a large bowl. Add the olive oil, lemon juice, mint, salt, and pepper. Taste and adjust seasonings, if needed.

Serve in bowls garnished with fresh mint (if using).

(V, GF)

SERVES 3

caesar salad with fried artichokes

Did you know that most caesar salad recipes aren't vegetarian? They usually have anchovies in the sauce. Here is my fish-free take on the classic salad. Subbing the fried artichokes for croutons really takes this to another level.

INGREDIENTS

1/4 c all purpose flour

1 large egg

1/2 c panko bread crumbs

6 tbsp grated parmesan; divided, plus more for garnish

1-14 oz can halved artichoke hearts, drained

5 tbsp extra virgin olive oil; divided

2 tbsp mayonaisse

2 tbsp lemon juice

1 tsp dijon mustard

1 clove garlic, grated

splash of pickle juice

2 romaine hearts, chopped

kosher salt and black pepper, to taste

DIRECTIONS

Place flour in a shallow dish. Lightly beat egg in another shallow dish. Combine panko and 4 tbsp of the parmesan in a third shallow dish.

Pat artichokes dry and toss in the flour to coat. Dip in the egg, letting the excess drop off. Roll into the panko mixture. Repeat with remaining pieces.

Heat 3 tbsp of the oil in a large nonstick skillet over medium heat. Add the artichoke hearts and cook, flipping once, until crispy and golden on both sides, 1-2 minutes per side. Transfer to a paper towel-lined plate.

For the salad dressing, whisk together the mayo, lemon juice, mustard, garlic, pickle juice, and remaining 2 tbsp each of olive oil and parmesan. Toss chopped romaine with the dressing. Season to taste with salt and pepper.

Serve topped with fried artichokes.

SERVES 6

watermelon & feta salad

This flavor combination is truly as good as it gets. The sweet watermelon mixed with the salty, tangy feta is just (insert chef's kiss gesture). Now I do have a secret to share here. I am a feta cheese snob. In my opinion, the only good feta cheese is the kind that comes in brine. All the others taste like what I assume packing foam tastes like.

INGREDIENTS

4 c, chopped watermelon

6 tbsp feta cheese, crumbled

one handful fresh mint leaves

DIRECTIONS

All you have to do is combine the ingredients and you're ready to eat! This is the easiest recipe in the whole book!

(GF)

SERVES 2

mediterranean rice salad

I'm really just giving away all my food truck secrets in this book, huh? This is another one of those salads that tastes even better the next day (and also another salad that I think maybe actually falls into the side dish category).

INGREDIENTS

3 c cold, cooked basmati rice

4 tbsp extra virgin olive oil

4 tbsp lemon juice

1 bunch parsley, chopped

1/2 c pitted, chopped kalamata olives

1/2 small red onion, finely chopped

3 roma tomatoes, finely chopped

6 mini bell peppers, finely chopped

1/3 english cucumber, finely chopped

1 tsp kosher salt, or to taste

2 tbsp zaatar

1 tbsp lemon pepper

1 tbsp minced garlic

5 tbsp feta, as garnish

DIRECTIONS

In a large bowl, combine the rice with the chopped parsley, olives, onion, tomatoes, peppers, and cucumber.

In a separate bowl, combine the olive oil, lemon juice, salt, zaatar, lemon pepper, and minced garlic. Once combined, pour into rice mixture and stir well to combine.

Serve garnished with crumbled feta cheese.

(GF)

SERVES 5-6

celebration salad

This is the perfect combination of a lunch salad and a fruit salad. You have sweet, savory, salty, and crunchy-all in one.

INGREDIENTS

5 oz container spring mix
1/2 c blueberries
1/2 c raspberries
1/3 c dried cherries
1/4 c chopped pecans or sunflower seeds
3/4 c strawberries, sliced
1/4 c sliced red onions
1/3 c feta cheese, crumbled
1 c croutons, for garnish

for the dressing:
2 tbsp extra virgin olive oil
1 tbsp honey
3 tbsp champagne vinegar
1/2 tsp kosher salt
1/4 tsp ground black pepper
1/4 tsp garlic powder

DIRECTIONS

In a small bowl, whisk together the olive oil, honey, vinegar, salt, pepper, and garlic powder. Set aside.

In a large serving bowl, combine the spring mix, blueberries, raspberries, dried cherries, pecans, strawberries, and onions, Add the dressing and mix well to combine.

Top evenly with feta cheese and croutons.

SERVES 4-6

MAINS

page 84: the famous leila's food truck falafel burger

page 87: spaghetti squash rounds

page 89: bbq jackfruit bowl

page 91: the mac & cheese to top all mac & cheeses

page 93: easy-peasy veggie chili

page 95: brunch casserole

page 97: kimchi fried rice

page 99: veggie stir-fry with tofu

page 103: peanut soba noodles

page 105: stuffed sweet potatoes

page 107: spinach alfredo pizza

page 109: gourmet grilled cheese

page 111: cheesy hash brown chili casserole

page 113: stuffed bell peppers

page 115: tacos with bread cheese, roasted potatoes & mango pico

page 117: baharan's eggplant lasagna

PHOTO CREDITS (CLOCKWISE FROM TOP LEFT): HAO TRAN, MCGRATH + MCKENNA DESIGN GROUP, BRAD HOLT, SHADAN KISHI PRICE

the famous leila's food truck falafel burger

Falafel is a common street food throughout the Middle East. When I started my food truck, I wanted to make it into the form of a burger patty versus the small ball-shaped kind you usually find. This version was so popular on my food truck that I ended up selling it as a frozen food item in stores. This recipe makes a big batch of them (see notes for how to freeze the extras). Not in a burger mood? This is also great for salads and wraps!

INGREDIENTS

1 c (uncooked) quick-cooking barley

1 tsp + 1 tbsp kosher salt, divided

2 tbsp ground flax seed

1 yellow onion, roughly chopped

1 large bunch parsley, roughly chopped*

1 large bunch cilantro, roughly chopped*

3- 15.5 oz cans chickpeas, rinsed and drained

6 tbsp lemon juice

1/2 tsp ground black pepper

1 tbsp garlic powder

2 tbsp ground cumin

2 tbsp zaatar

2 tbsp baking powder

1 c all purpose flour

3 c panko bread crumbs

extra virgin olive oil, for cooking

burger buns

assorted sauces and toppings

DIRECTIONS

Pour the barley and 1 tsp of the salt into a large heatproof bowl and cover with 4 c boiling water. Stir and then allow to sit until barley is cooked through (about 15 minutes). Drain off any remaining water very well and set aside until ready to use.

In a small bowl, combine the ground flax seed with 4 tbsp warm water. Stir to combine and set aside to thicken.

Meanwhile, in a large food processor, pulse together the onion, parsley, and cilantro until it's at a rough chop but not totally blended. Add the chickpeas and lemon juice and blend until everything is combined well. Add the pepper, garlic powder, cumin, zaatar, and the remaining 1 tbsp salt and process until it is all blended through (stopping to scrape down the bits at the sides of the bowl as needed). Add this mixture to the bowl of drained barley.

In that same mixing bowl, add the baking powder, flour, flax seed mixture, and panko. Combine everything until thoroughly mixed together. This mixture should be firm enough to hold it's shape when squeezed in your hand. If it is not that firm, add a small amount of flour at a time until you get that consistency.

(V)

the famous leila's food truck falafel burger (continued)

DIRECTIONS

If you are cooking the patties right away:

Pack a 1/2 c. scoop very firmly with this mixture and then level it to make sure patties are all the same size. Form that amount into a patty that is about 1/4" thick. Heat some oil in a skillet over medium heat and cook about 5 minutes per side or until browned on each side (let them sit them full time before flipping them over so they can form a crust.

If you are freezing the patties for later use:

Line the largest pan you have that will fit in your freezer with parchment paper. Pack a 1/2 c. scoop very firmly (and level it) with this mixture and then form that amount into a patty that is about 1/4" thick. Place this on the parchment paper and repeat with remaining mixture- leaving a little space between the patties (when the pan is full, set another sheet of parchment paper over top of those patties and do another layer as needed). Top all your layers with one more sheet of parchment and freeze overnight. Once they are frozen, you can combine them in a large storage bag, keeping some parchment between the layers so they don't stick together.

When you are ready to cook them, heat some oil in a skillet over medium heat and cook about 6 minutes per side or until browned on each side (let them sit them full time before flipping them over so they can form a crust.

A FEW HELPFUL TIPS BEFORE YOU START THIS RECIPE:

- THE STEMS HAVE FLAVOR TOO! I USE THE ENTIRE BUNCH, INCLUDING MOST OF THE STEMS. I ONLY CUT OFF ABOUT THE LAST INCH.

- USE A BURGER PRESS IF YOU HAVE ONE FOR AN EASIER TIME FORMING THE PATTIES.

- I USED A 14 CUP FOOD PROCESSOR. IF YOURS IS SMALLER, YOU WILL NEED TO BLEND TOGETHER THE INGREDIENTS IN BATCHES.

MAKES ABOUT 25 BURGER PATTIES

spaghetti squash rounds

It took me a minute to come around to spaghetti squash. First off, noodles are life. Secondly, I just never could get the texture right when I tried making it. That all changed with this recipe. Not only does slicing it in rounds make it easier and quicker to cook, it also just looks great.

INGREDIENTS

1 large spaghetti squash, cut into 1" thick rounds
2 tbsp extra virgin olive oil
1/2 tsp kosher salt
1/4 tsp ground black pepper
1- 10 oz pkg ground beef-style crumbles
1-24 oz jar marinara sauce
1 c (4 oz) shredded mozzarella or parmesan cheese
sliced basil, for garnish

DIRECTIONS

Preheat oven to 350 °F.

In the meantime, cut your spaghetti squash into 1" thick rounds. Then, using the rim of a drinking glass to assist you, cut out the seeds in the middle of each round.

Place these rounds on a parchment lined baking sheet and coat evenly with the olive oil, salt, and pepper.

Once the oven is ready, bake the rounds for 15-20 minutes or until soft enough to shred with a fork.

While the squash is roasting, cook the beef crumbles according to package instructions and then stir in the marinara sauce.

Once the squash is ready, remove from the oven and carefully pull the squash away from the outer ring until there is no more hole in the middle of each round. Evenly add the beef mixture and cheese on top of each round and bake an additional 5-10 minutes or until cheese is melted.

Garnish with the sliced basil.

SERVES 3-4

bbq jackfruit bowls

I make some variation of this dish at least once a month. The varieties are endless. This is also a great cookbook club dish because you can essentially set up a burrito bowl station with all sorts of toppings and let everyone customize their own. I save some time by using canned jackfruit, but if you're willing to deal with cutting up a fresh one- all the more power to you.

INGREDIENTS

1 large sweet potato, peeled and diced
2 tbsp extra virgin olive oil, divided
2 tsp garlic powder, divided
1 tsp kosher salt, divided
1/2 tsp smoked paprika
1- 14 oz can young jackfruit, drained and roughly chopped
1 tbsp barbecue sauce, or to taste
1- 15.5 oz can black beans, not drained
1 1/2 tsp onion powder, divided
1 tsp oregano
2 small (ripe) avocados, peeled, pitted, and roughly chopped
1 tbsp lemon juice
2 c chopped lettuce

DIRECTIONS

Preheat oven to 425 °F.

Place the diced sweet potatoes on a baking sheet lined with parchment paper. Top with 1 tbsp of the olive oil, 1/2 tsp garlic powder, 1/2 tsp kosher salt, and 1/2 tsp smoked paprika. Toss to combine and spread into a single layer. Bake 18-20 minutes, until potatoes are cooked through.

Meanwhile, heat the other tbsp of the olive oil in a skillet over medium heat. Add the chopped jackfruit and cook 10 minutes, stirring occasionally, until browned in spots. Reduce heat to low and add the barbecue sauce. Keep on low, stirring occasionally, until ready to assemble bowls.

For the black beans, pour the beans plus the liquid from the can in a small pot. Add 1 tsp onion powder, 1 tsp oregano, and 1 tsp garlic powder. Stir to combine and cook on the stovetop over medium-low heat, stirring occasionally, until ready to assemble bowls (drain cooking liquid before serving).

Lastly, make your avocado mixture. In a bowl, combine the avocado, 1 tbsp lemon juice, 1/4 tsp salt, 1/2 tsp garlic powder, and 1/2 tsp onion powder.

To serve, divide prepared foods among two bowls along with 1 c of chopped lettuce each.

(V)

SERVES 2-3

the mac & cheese to top all mac & cheeses

I have tried many a mac and cheese in my life. Through much trial and error, I have come to the conclusion that this is it's most superior form. The key is a little restaurant secret called sodium citrate which can easily be ordered online. Ever wonder how restaurants make those smooth, creamy sauces that don't split? Well, there you go. You're welcome. You can swap any of the cheeses out with another melting cheese but this combo is my favorite.

INGREDIENTS

for the mac:
1 1/4 c water
1 c whole milk
1 tbsp sodium citrate
8 oz muenster cheese, shredded
8 oz sharp cheddar cheese, shredded
8 oz pepperjack or hatch chile cheese, shredded
1 lb cellentani (corkscrew) pasta
kosher salt, to taste

for the (optional) topping:
1 c small cheese crackers
1 tbsp butter, chopped into a few pieces

DIRECTIONS

Combine sodium citrate in a pot with the water and milk. Bring to a simmer over medium heat, stirring occasionally with a whisk to dissolve. Add one of the shredded cheeses into the simmering liquid. Stir occasionally with whisk until mostly melted. Repeat in batches with remaining shredded cheeses. (It might seem like it's just not going to melt together at first but a few minutes of whisking will bring you the smooth texture you are looking for).

Meanwhile, cook pasta in salted, boiling water according to package directions. Drain, then add to your finished cheese sauce and mix well. Pour into a serving dish and serve immediately (or keep in pot on very low heat until ready to plate and serve).

***Want to make this dish even more over the top? Add this crispy, cheesy topping:

While the noodles are boiling, add the cheese crackers and butter pieces to a food processor and blend until it is coarsely combined (be careful not to over-blend). Set aside.

When pasta is done, place it in an oven-safe dish and top with the cracker mixture. Bake at 400 F for 10-15 minutes or until browned a bit on top.

SERVES 4-6

easy-peasy veggie chili

This is one of those dishes that I like to make when I have the time to make something in my slow cooker. If you don't have the time to wait around on a slow cooker, you can also cook this in a pot over medium-high heat and it will do the same job in about an hour.

INGREDIENTS

2 tbsp extra virgin olive oil

1 onion, chopped

1- 28 oz can crushed tomatoes

1 c salsa

1 tsp. chili powder

1 1/2 tsp ground cumin

1 tsp salt

1/4 tsp ground black pepper

1- 15 oz can black beans, rinsed and drained

1- 15 oz can kidney beans, rinsed and drained

1 red bell pepper, chopped

1 large zucchini, chopped

1 large squash, chopped

optional garnishes: cheese, avocado, radish, cilantro, jalapeno

DIRECTIONS

FOR STOVETOP:

Heat a dutch oven or heavy pot over medium heat and add the olive oil.

Add the onion, salt, and pepper and cook for 5 minutes or until onions have softened, stirring occasionally. Add the remaining ingredients and stir to combine.

Cover with lid slightly ajar, lower heat to medium-low, and cook 30-45 minutes or until vegetables are tender, stirring occasionally.

Ladle into bowls and top with optional garnishes.

FOR SLOW COOKER:

Combine all ingredients in slow cooker and mix well. Cook over high heat for about 4 hours or until vegetables are tender. (Stir occasionally, if possible).

Ladle into bowls and top with optional garnishes.

(V, GF)

SERVES 4-6

brunch casserole

This will be the star of any cookbook club. It's warm, filling, and so tasty. Want to take this dish and make it extra brunch-y? Add some sunny side eggs to the top towards the end of it cooking in the oven.

INGREDIENTS

1- 28 oz bag frozen tator tot rounds

1- 15 oz can condensed cream of portabello soup

2-10 oz packages ground beef-style crumbles

4 oz shredded cheddar cheese

4 oz shredded jack cheese

DIRECTIONS

Preheat oven to 450 °F.

Cook the beef crumbles according to package instructions in a cast iron skillet.

Meanwhile, in a small bowl, whisk together the condensed soup with water-according to package instructions.

Layer potatoes over the cooked beef, then evenly top with soup mix. Cover with the shredded cheeses.

Bake 30-45 minutes or until potatoes are cooked through.

SERVES 4-6

kimchi fried rice

Kimchi is Korean fermented cabbage. It's tangy and usually a little spicy (though mild versions are available too). One of my biggest regrets in life is that I only started eating kimchi in my mid-thirties. This recipe has been made a million ways by many people before me. This is how I like to make it.

INGREDIENTS

1-16 oz bag coleslaw mix
5 scallions, chopped
1 c (packed) kimchi; drained and chopped*
3 tbsp vegetable oil, divided
4 garlic cloves, finely chopped
2" piece of ginger, peeled and finely chopped
4 c chilled, cooked jasmine rice
2 tbsp toasted sesame oil
1/4-1/2 c soy sauce
6 eggs
sesame seeds and avocado, for garnish

*a note about kimchi: if you are sticking to a plant-based diet, make sure the kimchi you pick does not have any fish sauce or seafood paste in it.

DIRECTIONS

Heat 2 tbsp of the vegetable oil over medium heat in a wok. Cook the garlic, ginger, and scallions about 2 minutes, stirring often, until garlic is fragrant. Increase heat to medium high and add the cabbage mix and kimchi. Cook, stirring often, about 3-4 minutes or until cabbage is softened.

Add the cooked rice, sesame oil and 1/4 c of the soy sauce. Toss to combine. Press into an even layer in the wok and let cook, undisturbed, about 5 minutes, until slightly crisp underneath. Meanwhile, break 6 eggs into a bowl and whisk together with a small pinch of salt.

Push rice mixture to the side of the pan. Add the last tbsp of vegetable oil and add the eggs. Cook, stirring often, to a soft scramble. Once the eggs are ready, add to the rice mixture again and stir to combine. Taste for seasoning and add remaining 1/4 c soy sauce if desired.

Serve in bowls topped with sliced avocado and sesame seeds.

SERVES 4-6

veggie stir-fry with tofu

The stir-fry method of cooking originated in China- and what's better than throwing everything in the same pot and cooking it all together? This recipe is an example of what I usually like to add to mine- but most any vegetable works. Pro tip: bags of frozen stir fry veggies are usually very cheap. Keeping some on hand in your freezer makes this a quick, convenient meal any day of the week.

INGREDIENTS

3 tbsp vegetable oil, divided

1- 14 oz package extra firm tofu, drained

1/2 c cornstarch

2 tsp garlic powder

1 tsp everything bagel seasoning

2 1/2 tsp kosher salt, divided

1- 14.4 oz bag frozen stir fry vegetables

1 tbsp gochujang pepper paste (optional)

2- 3.5 oz packages sweet potato glass noodles

1- 15 oz can baby corn, drained

3 roma tomatoes, quartered

2 tbsp stir fry sauce, plus more to taste

optional topping: hot sauce

DIRECTIONS

Combine the cornstarch, garlic powder, everything bagel seasoning, and 1 tsp of the salt in a bowl. Mix well to combine and then set aside.

Pat your drained tofu with a paper towel to dry it off a bit but leave it a little wet so seasoning will adhere to it. Dice the tofu into cubes and then gently toss (a few pieces at a time) in the cornstarch mixture making sure all the sides get coated. Set seasoned tofu aside.

Heat 2 tbsp of the oil in a wok or nonstick skillet on medium heat. Once heated, cook the tofu until browned and crispy, about 5-8 minutes for each side. (Alternately, if you have an air fryer, you can just toss it all in there without the oil and bake them until crispy- giving them a shake halfway to loosen them up). Set cooked tofu aside.

*recipe continues on next page

SERVES 3-4

veggie stir-fry with tofu (continued)

DIRECTIONS

Set a small pot of water to boil.

In the meantime, carefully wipe out the wok, then add 1 tbsp of the oil. Set back on medium heat and let sit for one minute to heat up. Add the frozen vegetables and 1/2 tsp. salt. Stir to combine and cook 12-15 minutes, or until the vegetables are cooked through, stirring occasionally. (If you would like to add a little bit of heat to the dish, add in your gochujang in the last 2 minutes of cooking your vegetables, stirring occasionally to loosen it up and coat the vegetables evenly). Add in your quartered roma tomatoes and baby corn during the last 2 minutes of cooking so they can heat through.

While your vegetables are cooking, add 1 tsp salt to the boiling water and cook your noodles for 5 minutes, or until cooked through but not mushy. Drain the noodles set aside.

Once all the vegetables are ready (this should be around the same time the noodles are done) add the noodles to the wok and stir to combine. Add the stir fry sauce and reserved tofu and stir to combine again. You can add more stir fry sauce if you like your noodles more saucy.

Serve topped with hot sauce if you like it extra spicy!

(V)

HOW TO COOK A PERFECT JAMMY EGG

- BRING A POT OF WATER TO A BOIL OVER HIGH HEAT.

- CAREFULLY LOWER EGGS IN USING A SPOON.

- REDUCE HEAT TO MEDIUM-HIGH TO MAINTAIN A SIMMER.

- COOK EGGS FOR SEVEN MINUTES FOR THE PERFECT JAMMY EGG.

- DRAIN EGGS AND IMMEDIATELY PLACE INTO AN ICE BATH TO HALT COOKING.

peanut soba noodles

I don't know which is the star of this recipe- the noodles or the eggs? How does something so simple taste so good? Soba noodles are made of buckwheat flour and are a popular ingredient in Japanese cooking. They are a little chewy, yet firm and are often served cold.

INGREDIENTS

1- 9.5 oz pkg soba noodles

3 tbsp sesame oil

3 tbsp peanut butter

1 tbsp maple syrup, or to taste

3 tbsp soy sauce

3 tbsp rice vinegar

2 tsp garlic powder

3-4 jammy eggs, halved (see page 101 for directions)

1 english cucumber, half peeled and sliced

furikake seasoning, for garnish

DIRECTIONS

Cook noodles in salted, boiling water according to package instructions.

In the meantime, in a large bowl, whisk together the sesame oil, peanut butter, maple syrup, soy sauce, vinegar, and garlic powder. Set aside.

When noodles are done, drain and rinse under cold water to cool off noodles. Drain well and then add to your peanut sauce mixture. Stir well to combine.

Divide mixture among 3-4 bowls.

Add egg halves and sliced cucumber to each bowl. Top with furikake seasoning.

*Note: If your peanut butter is already sweetened, you may want to start with half of the maple syrup in your sauce and then add more to taste.

SERVES 3-4

stuffed sweet potatoes

Like the spaghetti squash, it took me a while to get on the sweet potato bandwagon. I usually prefer all things savory and the potato is no different. This is one of those recipes that finally won me over. It's a great dish that you can easily make a big batch of for party guests.

INGREDIENTS

1 sweet potato
1 tbsp extra virgin olive oil
1/2 tsp kosher salt
1/2 c cottage cheese
1 tbsp "everything but the bagel" seasoning
chopped fresh dill or parsley, to garnish

DIRECTIONS

Preheat oven to 425 °F.

Pierce your sweet potato a few times around with a fork. Coat evenly with the olive oil and salt.

Place the potato on a parchment lined baking sheet and bake for 40-50 minutes or until cooked through.

Cut a slit down the middle of the potato and carefully fluff the insides with a fork (be careful of the steam from the potato).

Top with the cottage cheese, seasoning, and some dill.

WANT A QUICKER VERSION OF THIS RECIPE?

Skip the oven and cook the sweet potato in the microwave. Pierce your sweet potato a few times around with a fork. Coat evenly with the olive oil and salt.

Microwave for 5 minutes, flipping halfway through the cooking time. If the sweet potato is not done after that, cook in 30 second intervals until cooked through.

(GF)

SERVES 1

spinach alfredo pizza

I present to you my take on one of my favorite takeout pizzas in town. Adding the second layer of cheese over the spinach keeps it from all burning up and gives it that great look.

INGREDIENTS

prepared pizza dough (see page 18)
flour, for rolling dough out
1 c alfredo sauce (see page 19)
2 c (8 oz) shredded pizza blend cheese
handful of spinach leaves
1 c (4 oz) grated parmesan cheese

DIRECTIONS

Preheat oven to 425 °F.

On a floured surface, roll out your prepared dough to about 1/4" thickness. Place the dough on a parchment lined baking sheet.

Spread alfredo sauce evenly over the dough, leaving about an inch all around for the crust.

Top with shredded pizza blend cheese, then spinach leaves, then parmesan cheese.

Bake for 15-20 minutes or until cheese is brown and bubbly in spots and dough is cooked through and lightly browned.

MAKES 1 LARGE OR 2 PERSONAL PIZZAS

★★★★★ 2 months ago

Man, I am a grilled cheese snob and I came out here on free comic book night wanting to try something new. Never knew honey and grapes could make a grilled cheese into a game changer, but damn it, I was wrong. Come to Denton for this amazing food!

P.S. the hummus and pita was fresh and delicious.

Right? I know it sounds strange at first but if they'd just take one damn bite then they'd be sold on it.

Delicious Much! I just had the best gourmet grilled cheese with honey and grapes and feta and muenster cheese! Jump back and kiss yoself it is so good! For real. Plus these gals are super nice. Stop by and tell them I sent you. #dentoning #leilasfoodtruckdenton #eatatleilas @leilastruck

leilastruck Thank you!!!! 🙂

Grilled cheese. Potato poppers. @leilastruck is sooo good! Gotta get that grilled cheese tho.

Leila's Food Truck best grilled cheese ever

gourmet grilled cheese

If cheese and grapes works on a charcuterie board, it stands to reason that it works as a grilled cheese as well. This was one of my most popular food truck offerings as you can see from the reviews on the previous page!

INGREDIENTS

1 tsp extra virgin olive oil
5 red grapes, halved
2 slices multigrain bread
2 oz shredded muenster cheese
1 tbsp crumbled feta cheese
1 tsp honey
1 tbsp unsalted butter, melted

DIRECTIONS

Heat olive oil in a skillet over medium heat. Add the halved grapes and cook for 4-5 minutes or until grapes soften a bit and get browned in spots.

In the meantime, add the muenster and feta cheeses to a slice of bread. Drizzle the honey over the cheese. When the grapes are ready, spread them evenly on your sandwich and top with the other slice of bread. Carefully wipe out the skillet to reuse for the sandwich and place back over medium-low heat.

Evenly brush the butter onto both sides of the sandwich and grill about 3 minutes per side or until golden brown and cheese is melted.

MAKES 1 SANDWICH

cheesy hash brown chili casserole

This is the casserole equivalent of a warm hug. Sometimes people think you can't have classic comfort foods without meat but if you feed them this dish, they likely won't make that comment again.

INGREDIENTS

4 tbsp extra virgin olive oil, divided
1 yellow onion, chopped
1 tbsp chili powder
2 tsp ground cumin
1 tsp smoked paprika
1 tsp garlic powder
2 tsp kosher salt, divided
1/4 tsp ground black pepper
1/4 c tomato paste
1-10 oz package ground chorizo-style crumbles
1- 15 oz can pinto beans, rinsed and drained
1-15 oz can diced tomatoes
1- 1 lb bag frozen shredded hash browns
2 c (8 oz) shredded cheddar cheese
parsley, for garnish

DIRECTIONS

Preheat oven to 400 °F.

Heat 2 tbsp of the olive oil in a skillet over medium heat. Add the onion, chili powder, cumin, smoked paprika, garlic powder, 1 tsp of the salt, and pepper. Cook until onions have softened, about 5 minutes, stirring occasionally.

Stir in the tomato paste and cook an additional minute. Add the chorizo crumbles and cook 3-4 minutes or until they are mostly cooked through, stirring occasionally. Add the beans and can of tomatoes (with their juices) and simmer 5 minutes to allow flavors to blend, stirring occasionally. Carefully transfer mixture to a 9x13 casserole dish and set aside.

In a large bowl, combine the shredded potatoes, cheese, 2 tbsp olive oil, and 1 tsp salt. Evenly spread this mixture on top of the casserole. Bake 35 minutes or until potatoes are cooked through.

SERVES 4-6

stuffed bell peppers

This is one of the first meals I learned how to cook myself. The fillings are endless but I personally love rice, beans, salsa, and cheese. This recipe is also great with large tomatoes as a substitute for the peppers, you just have to be very careful not to overcook them.

INGREDIENTS

6 bell peppers, assorted colors
2 tbsp extra virgin olive oil
1 tsp kosher salt
1-5.6 oz package Spanish rice mix
1- 15 oz can black beans, rinsed and drained
1 c salsa
1 or 1 1/2 c shredded cheddar, divided

DIRECTIONS

Preheat oven to 425 °F.

Cut bell peppers in half length-wise and remove seeds and some of the ribs (don't take off too much of the ribs as those are what allow the peppers to hold their shape). Place peppers on a parchment lined baking sheet (cut side down) and coat with the olive oil. Sprinkle salt on top. Roast peppers 20 minutes, or until they have started to soften but are not falling apart.

While the peppers are roasting, cook the Spanish rice according to package instructions. Once rice is cooked, stir in the salsa and the black beans. Remove from heat and set aside.

Once the peppers are ready, carefully flip them around on the baking sheet. Evenly fill each pepper with the rice mixture, then top with about 1/4 c each of the cheese.

Bake an additional 10 minutes or until cheese had melted.

SERVES 4-6

tacos with bread cheese, roasted potatoes & mango pico

Bread cheese is something I only recently discovered in the last few years. You can usually find it at your local grocery store but halloumi cheese is also a good swap for it. It has a firm outer texture but gets nice and gooey in the middle when you cook it. These tacos are just perfection.

INGREDIENTS

flour tortillas, warmed

10 oz bread cheese (or halloumi), cut into 1/2" wide strips

1 1/2-2 lb red potatoes, chopped

4 tbsp extra virgin olive oil, divided

1 1/2 tsp kosher salt

1 tbsp ground oregano

for mango pico:

2 mangoes, finely diced

1 jalapeno, seeded and finely diced

1 red bell pepper, finely diced

4 tbsp chopped cilantro

2 green onions, finely chopped

4 tbsp lime juice (about 2 limes)

1/2 tsp kosher salt, or to taste

DIRECTIONS

Preheat oven to 400 °F.

On a parchment lined baking sheet, coat the potatoes with 2 tbsp. of the olive oil, the salt, and the ground oregano. Bake for 15-20 minutes or until cooked through.

In the meantime, combine all your pico ingredients in a bowl and set aside to allow flavors to meld.

In a skillet, pour in the other 2 tbsp of olive oil and cook the slices of bread cheese over medium heat for about 2-3 minutes per side, or until browned on both sides and gooey and soft on the inside. Set aside.

Assemble the tacos in the warmed tortillas with the cheese, potatoes, and pico.

SERVES 3-4

baharan's eggplant lasagna

My sister and I are both obsessed with noodle dishes. This is one of her recipes that is always a crowd pleaser any time she makes it. It has both marinara sauce and a béchamel sauce that give it the perfect balance of flavors. Serve along with some garlic bread and a salad if you want to really go the extra mile.

INGREDIENTS

for eggplant marinara sauce:
2 medium eggplants, partially peeled and diced into 1/2" cubes
2/3 c tbsp extra virgin olive oil, divided
1 tsp kosher salt, divided
1 tsp garlic powder, divided
1/4 tsp ground black pepper, divided
2-24 oz jars marinara sauce; divided
1 tbsp sugar
1 tsp red pepper flakes
1/3 c red wine

*ingredients continue on next page

DIRECTIONS

Start by making your eggplant marinara sauce: Add 1/3 c of the olive oil to a large, high-sided nonstick pan over medium heat. Add the half of the diced eggplant, 1/2 tsp salt, 1/2 tsp garlic powder, and 1/8 tsp pepper. Saute, stirring occasionally, until eggplant is tender enough to mash with fork (about 10-15 minutes). Set this mixture aside and repeat process with other half of your diced eggplant.

To the pan of eggplant, carefully add the 2 jars of marinara (reserve 1 c worth and set aside), sugar, red pepper flakes, and the red wine. Cook for 5 minutes on medium heat, then reduce to a low simmer until ready to assemble the lasagna.

Next, you will want to make your béchamel sauce: In a saucepan over medium-low heat, whisk together the butter and flour, stirring frequently so flour doesn't burn, to form a roux (about 1 minute).

Carefully add in the milk, salt, pepper, and nutmeg. Let the mixture simmer, whisking occasionally to smooth out the sauce, about 8-10 minutes or until it has a thicker consistency (similar to an alfredo sauce). If it becomes too thick, add more milk. Remove from heat and set aside until you are ready to assemble the lasagna.

*recipe continues on next page

SERVES 6-8

baharan's eggplant lasagna (continued)

INGREDIENTS

for béchamel sauce:

1/4 c (half stick) unsalted butter, melted

1/2 c all purpose flour

2 c (16 oz) 2% milk, plus more as needed

1 tsp kosher salt

1/4 tsp ground black pepper

1 tsp ground nutmeg

for assembling:

1- 9 oz box "oven ready" or "no-boil" lasagna noodles

3 c (12 oz) shredded mozzarella

DIRECTIONS

Once you are ready to assemble the lasagna, turn the heat off of your sauces and preheat your oven to 375 °F.

In a 9x13 lasagna pan, add your reserved cup of plain marinara sauce (this helps keep the bottom from sticking to the pan). Evenly layer on your noodles, then 1/3 of the eggplant and béchamel sauces. Repeat this process two more times. Top lasagna evenly with the shredded mozzarella cheese.

Cover with foil and bake for 40 minutes. Uncover and continue baking 20-30 minutes more or until noodles are cooked through and cheese on top is browned and bubbly.

Allow lasagna to rest for about 15-20 minutes before serving.

DESSERTS

page 121: coconut-date bites
page 123: watermelon "cake"
page 125: ice cream with pistachio, saffron & rose
page 126: pomegranate molasses berry bowl
page 127: fruity frozen yogurt
page 129: chocolate chia mousse
page 131: pumpkin cake with cream cheese frosting
page 133: chocolate hazelnut cheesecake
page 135: berry cream pie
page 137: lemon cookie ice cream sandwiches
page 139: chocolate dipped citrus
page 141: saffron shortbread cookies

WE'RE FRIENDS BY THIS POINT OF THE BOOK, RIGHT? WELL, AS YOUR FRIEND, THERE IS SOMETHING I NEED TO TELL YOU:

YOU SPILLED SOMETHING ON YOUR SHIRT.

MADE YOU LOOK.

OK, BUT SERIOUSLY, I HAVE TO ADMIT THAT BAKING IS NOT MY THING. I DON'T REALLY CARE MUCH ABOUT SWEETS AND I LACK THE PATIENCE TO FOLLOW A RECIPE 100 % (IRONIC COMING FROM THE PERSON WHO WROTE THIS COOKBOOK, I KNOW). THE FOLLOWING DESSERT RECIPES ARE EITHER SUPER EASY TO MAKE OR WELL WORTH MUSTERING UP THE PATIENCE TO DO THEM CORRECTLY.

coconut-date bites

One last food truck recipe for the road. These are the perfect little sweet treat and healthy to boot! If you want to make them fancier, add some chopped nuts or seeds into the mix before rolling them into bites.

INGREDIENTS

1 lb pitted dates

1/3 c hot water

1 c shredded, sweetened coconut flakes; divided

1/8 tsp kosher salt

DIRECTIONS

Double check that all the pits have been removed from the dates (as well as the harder little round top part that is still on some of them)

Place them in a food processor along with the hot water, salt, and 1/4 c coconut flakes. Place mixture into a ball.

Form into heaping tbsp. bites and coat with remaining coconut. Refrigerate.

(V, GF)

MAKES ABOUT 20 BITES

watermelon "cake"

The hardest part of this recipe is making the whipped cream—which isn't hard at all. If you can get your hands on some edible flowers it is almost too pretty to eat. Almost.

INGREDIENTS

1" sliced round from a large watermelon

1 c heavy whipping cream

2 tbsp powdered sugar, or to taste

assorted berries, sliced fruits, edible flowers

lime zest, for garnish

DIRECTIONS

In a large bowl, whip the cream and powdered sugar together in a mixer on medium speed for a few minutes until it forms stiff peaks

Cut watermelon round into 8 wedges and place on a serving plate.

Spread whipped cream over the watermelon. Top with desired fruits and garnish with lemon zest.

(GF)

SERVES 8

ice cream with pistachio, saffron & rose

Go into any Iranian grocery store and you will be sure to find this ice cream flavor. You get to have two options here: the homemade version or the cheater's version. I'll let you choose your own adventure. A tip to anyone using rose water for the first time, a little goes a LONG way.

INGREDIENTS

2 c heavy cream

2 c whole milk

pinch of saffron (about 1/8 tsp)

3/4 c sugar

2 tsp vanilla extract

1/4 tsp kosher salt

1 tbsp rose water

1/2 c shelled, salted pistachios, roughly chopped; plus more for garnish

DIRECTIONS

In a small pot, cook cream, milk, saffron, and sugar over medium heat just enough for sugar to dissolve. Remove from heat.

Add vanilla extract, kosher salt, and rose water to the mixture. Let sit for 20 minutes at room temperature, then chill for 40 minutes in the refrigerator.

Pour mixture in an ice cream maker and process to desired texture (add chopped pistachios once ice cream has set a bit in the ice cream maker but still a little runny).

Serve garnished with more chopped pistachios.

(GF)

quicker version:

INGREDIENTS

1 pint vanilla ice cream, softened

pinch of saffron

1/4 tsp kosher salt

1 tbsp rose water

1/2 c pistachios, roughly chopped; plus more for garnish

DIRECTIONS

Let the ice cream soften enough to be able to mix in ingredients but not until it has melted. As soon as you are able, mix in the saffron, salt, rose water, and pistachios.

Re-freeze so that it hardens back to a regular ice cream texture.

Serve topped with chopped pistachios.

SERVES 4-6

pomegranate molasses berry bowl

Pomegranate molasses is back to save the day. This recipe is great with any berries you have on hand, especially the ones that are a little past their prime and need to be used up. Another pro tip if you want to be extra fancy: serve this along with some ice cream. So good!

INGREDIENTS

2 c mixed berries

1/3 c pomegranate molasses

DIRECTIONS

Wash berries and set aside to dry really well. Watery berries will dilute the flavor.

Once berries are dried, add the pomegranate molasses and gently stir to combine. Let sit for at least an hour for flavors to meld.

***This recipe is also great served alongside some ice cream.

(V, GF)

SERVES 2

fruity frozen yogurt

All you need for this recipe is a blender. Want to make this fun for cookbook club? Make your frozen yogurt and then set up a toppings bar for everyone to customize their own—just like in the stores. (Charging your friends per pound is up to you!)

INGREDIENTS

1-10 oz bag frozen fruit
2 tbsp honey (optional)
1/2 c plain or vanilla yogurt
1 tbsp lemon juice

DIRECTIONS

Add ingredients to blender or food processor and blend until smooth. (GF)

SERVES 2

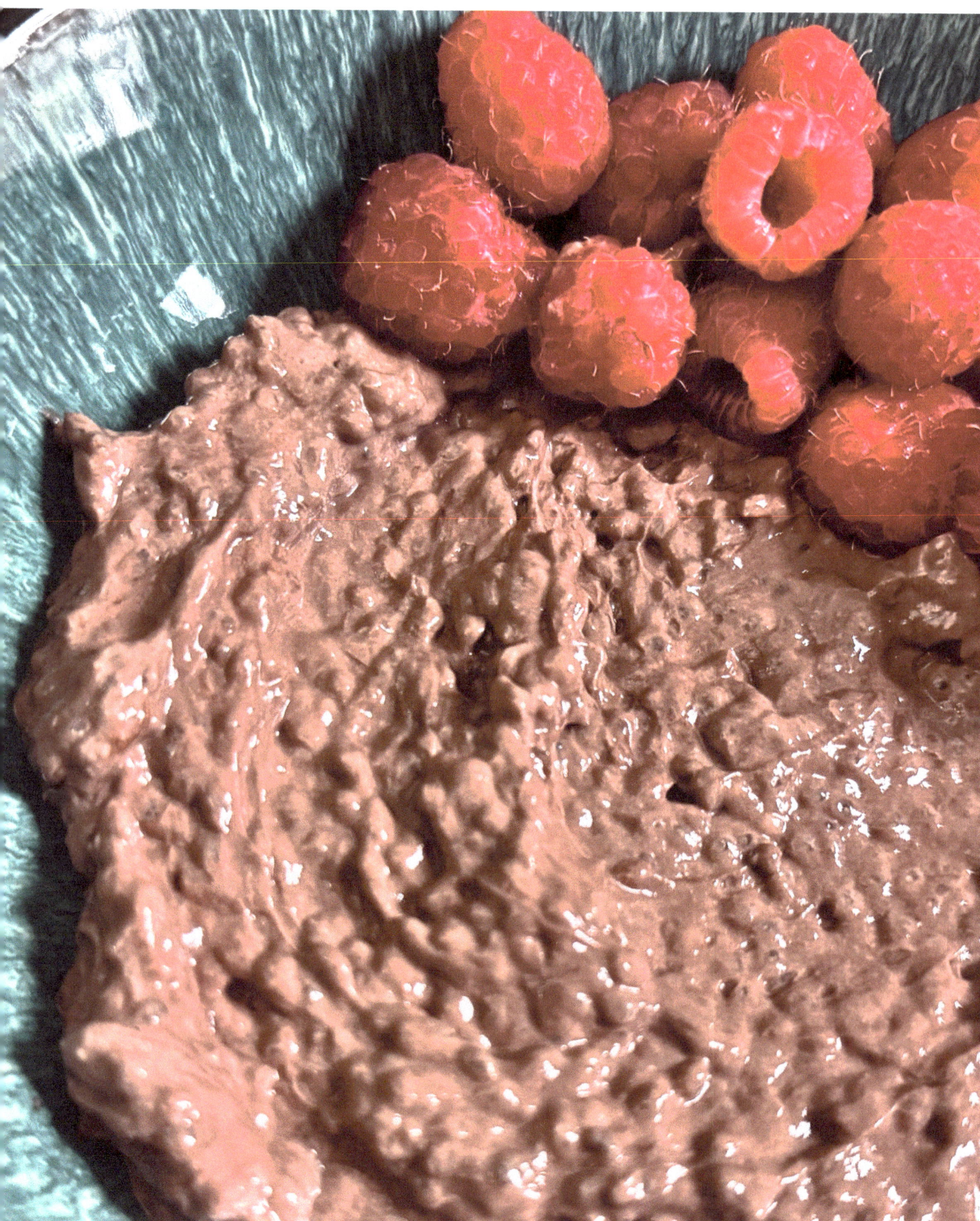

chocolate chia mousse

This is a decadent dessert that also ups your protein intake with the yogurt and chia seeds. It takes less than 5 minutes to assemble and just needs to sit in the fridge for a few hours to firm up.

INGREDIENTS

¾ c greek yogurt

1 c vanilla soymilk

2 tbsp maple syrup or honey

¼ c cocoa powder

¼ tsp kosher salt

⅓ c chia seeds

assorted toppings, for garnish (see directions for examples)

DIRECTIONS

In a bowl, whisk together the yogurt, soymilk, maple syrup, cocoa powder, and kosher salt. Once that is all combined, add in the chia seeds and whisk really well, trying to break up any clumps that may form.

At this point you can put this bowl directly in the fridge. For a nicer presentation, you can divide it up into smaller ramekins and then refrigerate.

Let it sit in the fridge for at least 2 hours or until firm.

Top with anything you would like. I like mine topped with berries, shredded coconut, or chocolate shavings.

(GF)

SERVES 4

pumpkin cake with cream cheese frosting

Now I do have to admit that I have much more experience eating this cake than baking it. This is the cake my mom makes me every year for my birthday. This will be sure to be a crowd pleaser. That cream cheese frosting mixed with the flavors of the cake is out of this world.

INGREDIENTS

for the cake:

4 eggs

3/4 c sugar

1 c vegetable oil

1 -15 oz can pumpkin puree

2 c all purpose four

2 tsp cinnamon

2 tsp baking powder

1 tsp baking soda

1 tsp kosher salt

for the frosting:

8 oz cream cheese, softened

1/2 c powdered sugar, or to taste

1/4 c fresh orange juice

1 tbsp orange zest

DIRECTIONS

Preheat oven to 350 °F.

Whisk together the flour, cinnamon, baking soda, baking powder, and salt. In another bowl, beat together sugar, eggs, oil, and pumpkin until well blended. Slowly add in the dry ingredients, mixing well. Pour into a greased 9x13 baking pan. Bake 25-30 minutes or until set. Allow to cool to room temperature before adding frosting.

To make the frosting, whip together the softened cream cheese, powdered sugar, orange juice, and orange zest until combined. Taste and add more sugar if desired.

Once the cake is ready, frost with your prepared cream cheese frosting.

WANT A QUICKER VERSION OF THIS CAKE?

Instead of baking the cake from scratch, use a boxed yellow cake mix. Cook according to directions except for reducing the water needed by half and adding 1 c of pumpkin puree.

SERVES 10-12

chocolate hazelnut cheesecake

Much to my sister's dismay—I'm not usually a huge fan of very chocolaty desserts. This recipe is an exception. It's so creamy and fluffy. It can be made as one big cheesecake or in small little clear single serve cups which would be easier for cookbook club.

INGREDIENTS

for the crust:

25 chocolate sandwich cookies

5 tbsp unsalted butter, melted

for the filling:

16 oz cream cheese, softened

1- 26.5 oz jars chocolate hazelnut spread

1 tsp vanilla extract

2 1/4 c heavy whipping cream

4 tbsp powdered sugar

chocolate shavings, for garnish

DIRECTIONS

Combine the cookies and butter in a food processor and pulse until it comes together in a course crumble (don't over-mix).

Tightly press the cookie mixture into a cheesecake pan lined with parchment paper for the crust. (The parchment paper allows you to easily remove it from the pan for serving. You don't need this if you are using single serve cups for serving instead of as a big cheesecake).

Clean and dry the food processor bowl to use again for filling. In it, combine the cream cheese, hazelnut spread, and vanilla extract. Blend until everything is combined, smooth, and creamy. Set aside.

In a mixer, whip the cream on medium speed with the sugar until it forms stiff peaks. Remove about a cup of the whipped cream to use as topping and set aside in the fridge. Fold in your chocolate mixture and mix just enough to combine (don't over-mix). Pour this mixture over the crust.

Cover with plastic wrap and place in the fridge at least 2 hours to set.

When you are ready to serve, add the reserved whipped cream on top and garnish with chocolate shavings.

SERVES 8

berry cream pie

My favorite flavor combination is sweet and salty. The saltines in the crust balance out the sweetness of the whipped cream and fruit to make the perfect pie. This dessert comes together so quickly and you can fold in whatever fruits you would like-the opportunities are endless. This recipe is my favorite way to make it.

INGREDIENTS

for the crust:

1 1/2 sleeves saltine crackers

1/2 c pecans

3 tbsp sugar

3/4 c (1 1/2 sticks) unsalted butter, softened

for the filling:

16 oz heavy whipping cream

3-4 tbsp powdered sugar, or to taste

1- 6 oz container raspberries (reserving a few for garnish)

1 pint blueberries (reserving about 1/4 c for garnish)

1- 16 oz container strawberries (reserving a few for garnish), diced

DIRECTIONS

In a food processor, combine the saltines and pecans to a coarse crumble. Add the 3 tbsp sugar and the butter and mix until well combined.

Press this crust mixture firmly into a greased pie pan and chill for 15 minutes.

Preheat oven to 350 °F.

Remove crust from fridge and bake for 18 minutes or until crust has browned a little on the edges. Set aside to cool to room temperature.

Meanwhile, whip the cream and powdered sugar together in a mixer on medium speed for a few minutes until it forms stiff peaks. Remove bowl from mixer and gently fold berries (make sure they are dried of any water) in with a spatula to combine. Set in the fridge until crust has cooled and is ready, then pour in the whipped cream mixture.

Garnish with more of the fruit on top and set in the fridge for up to an hour to harden a bit.

SERVES 8-10

lemon cookie ice cream sandwiches

If there is one things you will learn quickly about me, it is that I love lemons. Using the boxed cake mix makes these cookies super simple. They are the perfect softness to pair with the ice cream but still hold their shape.

INGREDIENTS

1 box "perfectly moist" lemon cake mix

2 lemons, zested

2 eggs

2 tbsp lemon juice

1/3 c vegetable oil

1 pint vanilla ice cream

DIRECTIONS

Preheat oven to 350 °F.

In a mixer, whisk blend together the cake mix, lemon zest, eggs, lemon juice, and vegetable oil to combine.

Add 8 level scoops (about ⅓ c. each) of your batter to a parchment lined baking sheet about an inch apart from each other. Bake cookies for 10-12 minutes or until starting to brown around edges but still a little soft in the middle. Remove cookies and allow to cool on a cookie rack.

About 20 minutes before you are ready to make the ice cream sandwiches, set the ice cream out to soften a bit. Flip 4 of the cookies over so the flat side is facing up. Place about ½ c. of ice cream in the middle of each of them and spread it out a bit without going to the edge of the cookies. Place the other cookies over the ice cream and gently press down to make sure the cookies are sticking together.

Serve immediately or store in freezer wrapped in parchment until ready to eat.

MAKES 4 COOKIE SANDWICHES

chocolate dipped citrus

This is a great recipe if you want to make something super simple that looks super fancy. These are very reminiscent of those chocolate covered citrus balls you see around the holidays. I like to use blood oranges but any type of orange would work great with this recipe.

INGREDIENTS

2 blood oranges, peeled and segmented
1/2 c dark chocolate chips
chopped almonds, to garnish

DIRECTIONS

Fill a small pot of water about 1/3 full of water and bring to a boil. In the meantime, get your chocolate in a heatproof boil that fits on top of the pot without touching the boiling water. Once the water is boiling, carefully place the bowl of chocolate over the pot and stir until chocolate is melted. This should only take about a minute or so.

In the meantime, line a plate or baking sheet with parchment paper.

Carefully remove the bowl of melted chocolate and set it aside.

Working with one segment at a time, dip a portion of the orange into the melted chocolate. Place this on the parchment paper and immediately sprinkle with come if the chopped almonds.

Repeat with remaining orange segments.

Transfer these to the refrigerator for about 15 minutes for them to firm up or until ready to serve.

(GF/ V depending on chocolate used)

SERVES 4

saffron shortbread cookies

These are great served along some hot tea or coffee. Saffron can be pricey so you can omit that ingredient and still have a tasty shortbread cookie. Get a little cookie stamp if you want to make them extra special.

INGREDIENTS

1 1/2 sticks (12 tbsp) unsalted butter, at room temperature
1/2 c powdered sugar
1/4 tsp kosher salt
1/2 tsp vanilla extract
tiny pinch (about 1/8 tsp) crushed saffron threads
1 1/2 c all purpose flour, plus more for rolling out

DIRECTIONS

In a small bowl, combine the crushed saffron with 1 tbsp of water. Stir to combine and let that sit for 5 minutes.

In a mixing bowl with a whisk attachment, combine the butter, sugar, salt, vanilla extract, and saffron water. Whisk on medium speed for about 30 seconds to combine. Add in your flour and whisk about a minute more until mixture comes together and flour is fully incorporated (you may need to stop the mixer and scrape down the bowl midway through). Place your dough ball in plastic wrap and refrigerate for 40 minutes.

Preheat oven to 350 °F.

Once the dough has chilled for 40 minutes, generously flour a clean surface and roll dough out to 1/4" thickness and cut out your shapes with a cookie cutter (the dough will be very soft and sticky-add more flour as needed if too soft to hold shape).

Place the cookies on a parchment lined baking sheet and bake 12-14 minutes or until light brown around the edges. Allow them to rest for about 15 minutes out of the oven for them to harden and cool down.

MAKES ABOUT 18- 2" COOKIES

GROCERY LIST

The following is a list of what I generally like to always keep in stock in my kitchen. You don't have to purchase these all at once, you can slowly add them to your regular kitchen staples.

REFRIGERATOR

ASSORTED CHEESES
ASSORTED CONDIMENTS
ASSORTED FRUITS
ASSORTED OLIVES
AVOCADO
BANANAS
BARBECUE SAUCE
BEETS
BELL PEPPERS
BROCCOLI
CAGE-FREE EGGS
CARROTS
CELERY
COTTAGE CHEESE
CUCUMBER
EGGPLANT
FRESH HERBS
GREEK YOGURT
HUMMUS
KIMCHI
LEMONS/LIMES
MAYONNAISE
MUSHROOMS
MUSTARD
NON-DAIRY MILK
PICKLES
RADISHES
ROMAINE LETTUCE
SALTED BUTTER
SCALLIONS
SPINACH
TOFU

PANTRY

ACTIVE DRY YEAST
ASSORTED CANNED BEANS
ASSORTED NUTS
ASSORTED PASTAS/NOODLES
ASSORTED POTATOES
ASSORTED VINEGARS
BASMATI RICE
BULGUR WHEAT
CANNED JACKFRUIT
CHIA SEEDS
COCONUT MILK
DATES
DICED TOMATOES
DOLMEH
EXTRA VIRGIN OLIVE OIL
FLOUR
GARLIC
HONEY
HOT SAUCE
LENTILS (DRY OR CANNED)
ONIONS
PASTA SAUCE
PEANUT BUTTER
ROSE WATER
SALSA
SEEDS (CHIA, FLAX)
SOURDOUGH BREAD
TOMATO PASTE
TOMATOES
VEGETABLE OIL
VEGETABLE STOCK CUBES

GROCERY LIST

HERBS & SPICES

BLACK PEPPER
CUMIN
GARLIC POWDER
KOSHER SALT
LEMON PEPPER
MINT
ONION POWDER
OREGANO
SAFFRON
SMOKED PAPRIKA
TACO SEASONING
ZAATAR

FREEZER

ASSORTED BERRIES
CONTAINER FOR VEGGIE SCRAPS (SEE PAGE 57)
CORN
EDAMAME
GROUND BEEF-STYLE CRUMBLES
POTATOES
STIR-FRY VEGETABLES

acknowledgments

This book was preceded by a million family dinners. Our family loves to get together and share a meal and I'm excited to be sharing these recipes with you so you can also share them with your friends and family.

To Trey, thank you for supporting my crazy ideas all the time and for washing way more dishes than any one person should probably ever have to wash.

To Maman and Baba, I could fill this whole book with thank you's to you both and it wouldn't scratch the surface. Maman, I hope to one day be able to make any dish taste as good as yours. Baba, thank you for all the Shirazi salads!

To Baharan, what do you mean you don't eat no meat?! (Inside joke, sorry). I'm sorry for making you sit on coolers in the minivan on family roadtrips so I could nap but I published a book with your name and pictures in it so we're even now, right?

To Joy, one day I will convince you that queso is amazing. Until that day, thank you for your suggestions and for bringing some Puerto Rican food into our lives.

To my extended family and friends, thank you all for the kind words and support—especially those of you who tested out recipes for me. I am my own worst critic, but thanks for being louder than what I hear in my head.

To my cookbook club group, thank you for coming over and letting me test all my recipes on you. Because of you, a lightbulb clicked in my head and I realized I needed to write this cookbook.

family dinners scrapbook

PHOTOS BY BAHARAN KISHI

index:

A

acknowledgements, 146
alfredo sauce, 19
appetizers & sides,
    Baked Feta w/ Roasted Tomatoes & Olives, 37
    Beet Hummus and Cottage Cheese Dip, 41-42
    Fried Olives in Yogurt Sauce, 29
    Joy's Cranberry Salsa, 31
    Labneh Bites, 27
    Pomegranate Glazed Eggplant, 39
    Potato Poppers w/ Two Sauces, 23
    Tomato-Mayo Toasts, 33
    Yogurt Stuffed Eggplant, 35
Artichoke & Basil Spread, 19
Ash Reshteh, 49

B

Baharan's Eggplant Lasagna, 117-118
Baked Feta w/ Roasted Tomatoes & Olives, 37
Basic Pizza Dough, 18
Basic Roasted Vegetables, 17
the basics,
    Alfredo Sauce, 19
    Artichoke & Basil Spread, 19
    Basic Pizza Dough, 18
    Basic Roasted Vegetables, 17
    Cholula Honey Butter, 20
    Citrus Vinaigrette Dressing, 15
    Everyday Salad Dressing, 15
    Lemony Pesto Sauce, 16
    Marinara Sauce, 19
    Not-So-Secret Burger Sauce, 16
    Pickled Onions, 16
    Sumac Onions, 16
    Taco Seasoning, 20
Bbq Jackfruit Bowl, 89
beans,
    Ash Reshteh, 49
    Bbq Jackfruit Bowl, 89
    Beet Hummus, 41
    Cheesy Hash Brown Chili Casserole, 111
    Chickpea Noodle Soup, 47
    Easy-Peasy Veggie Chili, 93
    Famous Leila's Food Truck Falafel Burger, 84-85
    Minestrone Soup w/ Tortellini, 59
    Stuffed Bell Peppers, 113
    White Bean and Kale Soup, 51
Beet Hummus, 41
Beet Yogurt Sauce, 25
beets,
    Beet Hummus, 41
    Beet Yogurt Sauce, 25
bell peppers,
    Baked Feta w/ Roasted Tomatoes & Olives, 37
    Basic Roasted Vegetables, 17
    Stuffed Bell Peppers, 113
Berry Cream Pie, 135
bowls,
    Bbq Jackfruit Bowl, 89
    Pomegranate Molasses Berry Bowl, 126
Broccoli & Feta Soup, 45
Brunch Casserole, 95
burgers,
    Cheeseburger Salad, 71
    Famous Leila's Food Truck Falafel Burger, 84-85
    Not-So-Secret Burger Sauce, 16

C

Caesar Salad w/ Fried Artichokes, 75
casseroles,
    Brunch Casserole, 95
    Cheesy Hash Brown Chili Casserole, 111
Celebration Salad, 81
cheese,
    Baharan's Eggplant Lasagna, 117-118
    Baked Feta w/ Roasted Tomatoes & Olives, 37
    Broccoli & Feta Soup, 45
    Cheeseburger Salad, 71
    Cheesy Hash Brown Chili Casserole, 111
    Chocolate Hazelnut Cheesecake, 133
    Feta & Cream Cheese Sauce, 24
    Gourmet Grilled Cheese, 109
    The Mac & Cheese to Top All Mac & Cheeses, 91
    Pumpkin Cake w/ Cream Cheese Frosting, 131
    Tacos w/ Bread Cheese, Roasted Potatoes, & Mango Pico, 115
    Tomato Soup w/ Grilled Cheese Croutons, 55-56
    Watermelon & Feta Salad, 77
Cheeseburger Salad, 71

Cheesy Hash Brown Chili Casserole, 111
chickpeas,
- Ash Reshteh, 49
- Beet Hummus, 41
- Chickpea Noodle Soup, 47
- Famous Leila's Food Truck Falafel Burger, 84-85

Chickpea Noodle Soup, 47
chili,
- Cheesy Hash Brown Chili Casserole, 111
- Easy-Peasy Veggie Chili, 93

chocolate,
- Chocolate Chia Mousse, 129
- Chocolate Dipped Citrus, 139
- Chocolate Hazelnut Cheesecake, 133

Chocolate Chia Mousse, 129
Chocolate Dipped Citrus, 139
Chocolate Hazelnut Cheesecake, 133
Cholula Honey Butter, 20
citrus,
- Chocolate Dipped Citrus, 139
- Citrus Vinaigrette Dressing, 15
- Lemon Cookie Ice Cream Sandwiches, 137

Citrus Vinaigrette Dressing, 15
coconut,
- Coconut Soup w/ Tofu, 53
- Coconut-Date Bites, 121

Coconut Soup w/ Tofu, 53
Coconut- Date Bites, 121
Cookbook Club (what is), 3
cottage cheese,
- Cottage Cheese Dip, 42
- Stuffed Sweet Potatoes, 105

Cottage Cheese Dip, 42

D

desserts,
- Berry Cream Pie, 135
- Chocolate Chia Mousse, 129
- Chocolate Dipped Citrus, 139
- Chocolate Hazelnut Cheesecake, 133
- Coconut-Date Bites, 121
- Fruity Frozen Yogurt, 127
- Ice Cream w/ Pistachio, Saffron & Rose, 125
- Lemon Cookie Ice Cream Sandwiches, 137
- Pomegranate Molasses Berry Bowl, 126
- Pumpkin Cake w/ Cream Cheese Frosting, 131
- Saffron Shortbread Cookies, 141
- Watermelon "Cake," 123

dressings,
- Citrus Vinaigrette Dressing, 15
- Everyday Salad Dressing, 15

E

Easy-Peasy Veggie Chili, 93
eggplant,
- Baharan's Eggplant Lasagna, 117-118
- Pomegranate Glazed Eggplant, 39
- Yogurt Stuffed Eggplant, 35

eggs,
- Peanut Soba Noodles, 103
- Perfect Jammy Egg, 101

Everyday Salad Dressing, 15

F

Famous Leila's Food Truck Falafel Burger, 84-85
feta,
- Baked Feta w/ Roasted Tomatoes & Olives, 37
- Broccoli & Feta Soup, 45
- Feta & Cream Cheese Sauce, 24
- Watermelon & Feta Salad, 77

Feta & Cream Cheese Sauce, 24
fried foods,
- Caesar Salad w/ Fried Artichokes, 75
- Fried Olives in Yogurt Sauce, 29
- Potato Poppers w/ Two Sauces, 23

Fried Olives in Yogurt Sauce, 29
fruit,
- Berry Cream Pie, 135
- Coconut-Date Bites, 121
- Fruity Frozen Yogurt, 127
- Kale and Fruit Salad, 69
- Pomegranate Molasses Berry Bowl, 126
- Tacos w/ Bread Cheese, Roasted Potatoes & Mango Pico, 115
- Watermelon "Cake," 123
- Watermelon & Feta Salad, 77

Fruity Frozen Yogurt, 127

G

Gourmet Grilled Cheese, 109
grocery list, 144-145

H

I

Ice Cream w/ Pistachio, Saffron & Rose, 125
introduction, 1-2

J

Joy's Cranberry Salsa, 31

K

kale,
    Kale and Fruit Salad, 69
    White Bean and Kale Soup, 51
Kale and Fruit Salad, 69
Kimchi Fried Rice, 97

L

Labneh Bites, 27
Lemon Cookie Ice Cream Sandwiches, 137
Lemony Pesto Sauce, 16

M

The Mac & Cheese to Top All Mac & Cheeses, 91
main dishes,
    Baharan's Eggplant Lasagna, 117-118
    Bbq Jackfruit Bowl, 89
    Brunch Casserole, 95
    Cheesy Hash Brown Chili Casserole, 111
    Easy-Peasy Veggie Chili, 93
    Famous Leila's Food Truck Falafel Burger, 84-85
    Gourmet Grilled Cheese, 109
    Kimchi Fried Rice, 97
    The Mac & Cheese to Top All Mac & Cheeses, 91
    Peanut Soba Noodles, 103
    Spaghetti Squash Rounds, 87
    Spinach Alfredo Pizza, 107
    Stuffed Bell Peppers, 113
    Stuffed Sweet Potatoes, 105
    Tacos w/ Bread Cheese, Roasted Potatoes & Mango Pico, 115
    Veggie Stir-Fry with Tofu, 99-100
Maman's Pasta Salad, 65
Marinara Sauce, 19
Mediterranean Rice Salad, 79
Minestrone Soup w/ Tortellini, 59

N

noodles/pastas,
    Ash Reshteh, 49
    Baharan's Eggplant Lasagna, 117-118
    Broccoli & Feta Soup, 45
    Chickpea Noodle Soup, 47
    The Mac & Cheese to Top All Mac & Cheeses, 91
    Maman's Pasta Salad, 65
    Minestrone Soup w/ Tortellini, 59
    Peanut Soba Noodles, 103
    Veggie Stir-Fry w/ Tofu, 99-100
    White Bean and Kale Soup, 51
Not-So-Secret Burger Sauce, 16

O

P

pastas/noodles,
    Ash Reshteh, 49
    Baharan's Eggplant Lasagna, 117-118
    Broccoli & Feta Soup, 45
    Chickpea Noodle Soup, 47
    The Mac & Cheese to Top All Mac & Cheeses, 91
    Maman's Pasta Salad, 65
    Minestrone Soup w/ Tortellini, 59
    Peanut Soba Noodles, 103
    Veggie Stir-Fry w/ Tofu, 99-100
    White Bean and Kale Soup, 51
Peanut Soba Noodles, 103
Perfect Jammy Egg, 101
Pickled Onions, 16
pickled vegetables,
    Pickle Onions, 16
    Sumac Onions, 16
pizza,
    Basic Pizza Dough, 18
    Spinach Alfredo Pizza, 107
plant-based cooking (what are), 5
pomegranate,
    Pomegranate Glazed Eggplant, 39

Pomegranate Molasses Berry Bowl, 126
Yogurt Stuffed Eggplant, 35
Pomegranate Glazed Eggplant, 39
Pomegranate Molasses Berry Bowl, 126
potatoes,
- Brunch Casserole, 95
- Cheesy Hash Brown Chili Casserole, 111
- Potato Poppers w/ Two Sauces, 23
- Seattle Chowder, 61-62
- Stuffed Sweet Potatoes, 105
- Tacos w/ Bread Cheese, Roasted Potatoes & Mango Pico, 115

Potato Poppers w/ Two Sauces, 23
Pumpkin Cake w/ Cream Cheese Frosting, 131

Q

R

rice,
- Kimchi Fried Rice, 97
- Mediterranean Rice Salad, 79

S

saffron,
- Ice Cream w/ Pistachio, Saffron & Rose, 125
- Saffron Shortbread Cookies, 141

Saffron Shortbread Cookies, 141
Salad Shirazi, 73
salads,
- Caesar Salad w/ Fried Artichokes, 75
- Celebration Salad, 81
- Cheeseburger Salad, 71
- Kale and Fruit Salad, 69
- Maman's Pasta Salad, 65
- Mediterranean Rice Salad, 79
- Salad Shirazi, 73
- Tabbouli, 67
- Watermelon & Feta Salad, 77

sandwiches,
- Gourmet Grilled Cheese, 109
- Lemon Cookie Ice Cream Sandwiches, 137
- Tomato-Mayo Toasts, 33
- Tomato Soup w/ Grilled Cheese Croutons, 55-56

sauces,
- Alfredo Sauce, 19
- Beet Yogurt Sauce, 25
- Feta & Cream Cheese Sauce, 24
- Lemony Pesto Sauce, 16
- Marinara Sauce, 19
- Not-So-Secret Burger Sauce, 16

Seattle Chowder, 61-62
a "souper" tip, 57
soups,
- Ash Reshteh, 49
- Broccoli & Feta Soup, 45
- Chickpea Noodle Soup, 47
- Coconut Soup w/ Tofu, 53
- Minestrone Soup w/ Tortellini, 59
- Seattle Chowder, 61-62
- Tomato Soup w/ Grilled Cheese Croutons, 55-56
- White Bean and Kale Soup, 51

Spaghetti Squash Rounds, 87
Spinach Alfredo Pizza, 107
Stuffed Bell Peppers, 113
Stuffed Sweet Potatoes, 105
Sumac Onions, 16

T

Tabbouli, 67
tacos,
- Taco Seasoning, 20
- Tacos w/ Bread Cheese, Roasted Potatoes & Mango Pico, 115

Taco Seasoning, 20
Tacos w/ Bread Cheese, Roasted Potatoes & Mango Pico, 115
theme ideas, 8-12
tinkletown (inside joke. You happy now Quigs?)
tips,
- A "Souper" Tip, 57
- Tips for Success, 6-7

tips for success, 6-7
tofu,
- Coconut Soup w/ Tofu, 53
- Veggie Stir-Fry w/ Tofu, 99-100

tomatoes,
- Baked Feta w/ Roasted Tomatoes & Olives, 37
- Tomato Soup w/ Grilled Cheese Croutons, 55-56
- Tomato-Mayo Toasts, 33

Tomato Soup w/ Grilled Cheese Croutons, 55-56

Tomato-Mayo Toasts, 33

U

V

Veggie Stir-Fry w/ Tofu, 99-100

W

Watermelon "Cake," 123
Watermelon & Feta Salad, 77
White Bean and Kale Soup, 51

X

Y

yogurt,
    Beet Yogurt Sauce, 25
      Fried Olives in Yogurt Sauce, 29
      Yogurt Stuffed Eggplant, 35
Yogurt Stuffed Eggplant, 35

Z

www.ingramcontent.com/pod-product-compliance
Lightning Source LLC
Chambersburg PA
CBHW061129170426
43209CB00014B/1712